How To L
Intergove

Univer

How To Lobby at Intergovernmental Meetings

Mine's a Caffè Latte

by Felix Dodds
with Michael Strauss

STAKEHOLDER FORUM

London • Sterling, VA

First published by Earthscan in the UK and USA in 2004
Reprinted 2006

ISBN-10: 1-84407-074-3
ISBN-13: 978-1-84407-074-9

Typesetting by MapSet Ltd, Gateshead, UK
Printed and bound in the UK by Bath Press
Cover design by Declan Buckley

For a full list of publications please contact:

Earthscan
8–12 Camden High Street
London, NW1 0JH, UK
Tel: +44 (0)20 7387 8558
Fax: +44 (0)20 7387 8998
Email: earthinfo@earthscan.co.uk
Web: **www.earthscan.co.uk**

22883 Quicksilver Drive, Sterling, VA 20166-2012, USA

Earthscan publishes in association with the International Institute for
Environment and Development

A catalogue record for this book is available from the British Library

Library of Congress Cataloging-in-Publication Data

Dodds, Felix.
How to lobby at intergovernmental meetings / by Felix Dodds with Michael
Strauss.
    p. cm.
  ISBN 1-84407-074-3 (pbk.)
    1. International agencies. 2. Lobbying. I. Strauss, Michael, 1952- II. Title
JZ4850.D63 2003
324'.4—dc22

                                                          2003017969

Contents

List of Figures, Tables and Boxes

FIGURES

TABLES

BOXES

About the Authors

Felix Dodds is the executive director of Stakeholder Forum for Our Common Future. He was co-chair of the Commission on Sustainable Development (CSD) NGO Steering Committee from 1997 to 2001. He has been active at all UN Commission on Sustainable Development meetings, as well as a number of other UN commissions. He attended the Earth Summit in Rio in 1992, the second United Nations Conference on Human Settlements (Habitat II) in Istanbul in 1996 and the World Summit on Sustainable Development (WSSD or Earth  Summit 2002) in Johannesburg in 2002, as well as the five-year follow-ups (+5s) for Rio, Beijing and Copenhagen. He coordinated NGO lobbying at Habitat II in 1996 and Rio +5 in 1997. His previous books are *Earth Summit 2002: A New Deal* (Earthscan, 2001), *The Way Forward Beyond Agenda 21* (Earthscan, 1997) and *Into the 21st Century: An Agenda for Political Realignment* (Green Print, 1988). He has also contributed chapters to a number of other books. He has two children, Robin and Merri, who are loads of fun to be with.

Felix Dodds, Executive Director
Stakeholder Forum for Our Common Future
7 Holyrood Street, London, SE1 2EL, UK
Tel: +44 (0)20 7089 4300
Fax: +44 (0)20 7089 4310
Email: fdodds@stakeholderforum.org
Website: www.stakeholderforum.org

Michael Strauss is founder and executive director of Earth Media, a political and media consultancy that works with international and national NGOs and coalitions on environmental, economic development and social justice issues. He has organized press events at the UN since the 1992 Earth Summit in Rio, and has served as media consultant for organizations in New York, Copenhagen, Brussels, London and Paris. At the 2002 Johannesburg Summit he was selected by the UN to coordinate the daily press conference and publicity for NGO coalitions in the UN Media Centre at Sandton Convention Centre. He was media coordinator for the CSD NGO Steering Committee from 1993 to 2001. He is editor of *The Dialogue Records: Year One* (Northern Clearinghouse, 1999).

For information on NGO coalition media activities or advice on other press areas, contact:

Michael Strauss, Executive Director
Earth Media
320 East 54th Street, 3H, New York, NY 10022, USA
Tel: +1 212 355 2122
Email: earthmedia@igc.org

Foreword

A long-standing relationship between the UN and Felix Dodds has given him the authority and the experience to bring the reader closer to one of the remarkable inventions of the 20th century. The book is a tribute to this human institution, with its frailties and limitations, albeit invested with the hopes and confidence of the common individual, and also to the steady rise and influence of organized world society in the way that it functions. Felix Dodds shares with the reader his vision of how the UN concept can become reality in the 21st century, thus fulfilling the multilateral dream of peace and justice.

In describing its breadth, length and height, from its addresses and physical facilities to its intricate structure and framework that reach, in encyclopaedic fashion, every possible subject, resource and problem that is of interest to mankind, the book is a practical guide to its players, rituals and procedures. What sound like simple hints drawn from day-to-day experience are, in fact, remarkable lessons to be learned that may have been inspired by Niccolò Machiavelli, Emily Post or Carl von Clausewitz. Tactical moves, a strong feeling for the importance of language, and a keen sense of organization are other valuable insights that aim at effective action and results in the best sense of the term.

The reader may start out referring to the UN in the third-person singular, but may well, at the end, think of it in the first-person plural.

Henrique B Cavalcanti
President, Intergovernmental Forum on Chemical Safety
former Minister of Environment and the Amazon, Brazil
Chair, UN Commission on Sustainable Development, 1995

Preface

We must always tell them that they are not alone, their action is not futile, there always comes a day when the palaces of oppression crumble, when imprisonment comes to an end, when liberty catches fire.

(Albert Camus)

This book started life as a briefing document for stakeholders involved in the World Summit on Sustainable Development (WSSD), otherwise known as Earth Summit 2002. The briefing was very popular during the WSSD process and it seemed to many people that a book would help newcomers and organizations in their engagement at the inter-governmental level, no matter what their purpose for being involved.

The book has drawn both on suggestions by many individuals whom I have listed in the acknowledgements section, as well as Stakeholder Forum for Our Common Future's ten years of experience in lobbying at the UN level on sustainable development. Despite this background, a lot of the book is interchangeable. You could replace 'stakeholder' with 'governments' and the information would be relevant to government delegations. Just like stakeholders, governments are trying to get their positions accepted by as many decision-makers as possible. Much of the book can also be used for national campaigning.

Over the past 30 years since the Stockholm UN Conference on the Human Environment, non-governmental organizations (NGOs), and stakeholders[1] generally, have played an increasingly influential and constructive role in framing the direction that the world might go in. Understanding how to lobby more effectively helps to deepen democracy and promote greater dialogue and richness of perspectives in the intergovernmental process. Although we have finished a sequence of UN conferences and summits, this does not mean the end of intergovernmental decision-making. The monitoring of government commitments at the intergovernmental level is critical to the phase that we are now in.

I would like to dedicate the book to Warren Lindner ('Chip' to his friends), who died of an AIDS-related illness during the preparatory process for the WSSD. He had been secretary of the Brundtland Commission and organizer of the Rio Global Forum in 1992. The Stakeholder Forum for Our Common Future took its name out of respect for his work and his previous organization, the Centre for Our Common Future. We do this to honour the work of a departed colleague who gave much of his life to try, at the intergovernmental level, to work for a more sustainable world.

When times seem difficult, and they will be, it is good to have in mind something that John F Kennedy said in his inaugural speech: 'Let us never negotiate out of fear. But let us never fear to negotiate.'

Suggestions for improving this resource will be welcomed at: info@stakeholderforum.org.

Felix Dodds
Osterley, November 2003

Key Messages[1]

- **Know Your Own Goals**
  Decide, define and describe your objective(s) in a form that others can understand and will want to read. This is essential, however and wherever you wish to advance a particular issue.

- **Know the Decision-making Process in Your Country**
  Study, understand and respect the decision-making process. Identify how, where and when decisions relating to your objective(s) will be taken.

- **Know When To Work at What Level**
  It is important to be clear about when to be active at the national level and when to be active at the international level. Do not confuse what can be done at either level.

- **Know the Decision-making Context**
  Study the wider political context in which decisions are being taken. Ministers have limited time, and priorities are continually shifting. Are there ways in which you can raise the priority of an issue? Are there natural cycles when the issue comes to the fore?

- **Know the Tools at Your Disposal**
  What are the most cost-effective means of communicating your message? The internet has become a cheap and accessible means of delivering messages, and supplements the print and electronic media.

- **Know When To Make Your Position**
  Understand the diary of decision-making. When do you need to have your ideas in front of officials for them to be considered? Last

minute proposals are rarely successful: it usually takes time, persistence and a willingness to learn in order to win.

- **Know Your Allies**
  Identify who can help share, amplify or adopt your objective(s), and those who might join in a coalition around the issue. This will help to strengthen your case and argument. Sometimes allies are inside the process (for example, other stakeholders); sometimes they are outside (for example, the media or the judiciary). Define the terms and duration of alliances carefully.

- **Know the Government Officials**
  Identify who the key governments are and who their key officials are. Meet them and buy them coffee!

- **Know the Key UN Officials**
  Identify who is playing a key role within the relevant secretariats and within the UN agencies and programmes.

- **Know Your Adversaries**
  Know why others differ from your viewpoint. Address their concerns in developing your position. This will also strengthen your case.

- **Know Your Limits**
  You will not have all the answers: be prepared to acknowledge this. Coalitions mean compromise: be prepared to adopt others' viewpoints if you expect them to adopt yours. Compromise does not necessarily mean a weaker position.

- **Know Your Potential**
  Historically, activism has been a major factor in driving change for the better. A few people armed with the right idea, conviction and courage can change the world. The challenge is to find the few words and actions that ignite people's imaginations.

- **Know Your Brackets and Terms**
  Why are governments using certain terms? Why are they bracketing particular sections? You need to know the answers to these questions in order to know what your action should be.

Acknowledgements

We would like to thank the following people who commented on the drafts of this book and those who gave their support for this project. Thanks: Peter Adriance, Georgina Ayre, Jeffrey Barber, Sander van Bennekom, Karen Birdsall, Alexandra Biod, Madeleine Cobb, Derek Dodds, Robin Dodds, Kevin Dunion, Maria Figueroa, David Fitzpatrick, Beth Hiblin, Paul Hohnen, Leif Holmberg, Megan Howell, Laura Kallus, Geeta Kulshrestha, Chris Littlecott, Suzanne Long, Bill Mankin, Toby Middleton, Daniel Mittler, Aretha Moore, Goodwin Ojo, Peter Padbury, Gary Pupurs, Bunker Roy, and Lucien Royer.

List of Acronyms, Abbreviations and General Terms

ACABQ	Advisory Committee on Administrative and Budgetary Questions
ACC	Administrative Committee on Coordination (UN Secretary-General's Cabinet)
ANPED	Northern Alliance for Sustainability
AOSIS	Alliance of Small Island States (42 members and observers)
ATO	Arab Towns Organization
BASD	Business Action for Sustainable Development
BCSD	Business Council for Sustainable Development
bureau	the bureau of a commission is composed of the chair and representatives of the other five regional groupings of member states
CAN	Climate Action Network
CARICOM	Caribbean community: Antigua and Barbuda, Bahamas, Barbados, Belize, Dominica, Grenada, Guyana, Jamaica, Saint Kitts and Nevis, Saint Lucia, Saint Vincent and the Grenadines, Trinidad and Tobago
CBD	Convention on Biological Diversity
CCD	Convention to Combat Desertification
CEDAW	Committee on the Elimination of Discrimination against Women
CEE	Central and Eastern Europe
chair	the chair is responsible for facilitating progress in

	the work of the meeting; during a commission, they serve from the end of the previous session until the end of the one that they are chairing; different chairs may be elected for other informal groups
CHS	Commission on Human Settlements
CITES	Convention on International Trade in Endangered Species of Wild Fauna and Flora
City Summit	see Habitat II
CO_2	carbon dioxide
COP	Conference of the Parties (to a convention)
COREPER	EU Committee of Permanent Representatives
COW	Committee of the Whole
CPD	Commission on Population and Development
CSD	Commission on Sustainable Development (53 member state governments make up the commission, which meets annually; observer states and non-members (such as the EU) are also permitted to attend)
CSO	civil society organization
CSocD	Commission for Social Development
CTE	Committee on Trade and Environment (of the WTO)
DAW	UN Division for the Advancement of Women
DESA	UN Department of Economic and Social Affairs (responsible for many of the commissions that deal with reviewing implementation of the outcomes from the summits and conferences of the 1990s; run by an under secretary-general)
DM	UN Department of Management
DPA	UN Department of Political Affairs
DPI	UN Department of Public Information
DPKO	UN Department of Peace-keeping Operations
DSD	UN Division for Sustainable Development (division of ECOSOC, concerned with sustainable development issues; the DSD acts as the secretariat for the CSD)
DSPD	UN Division for Social Policy and Development (division of ECOSOC, concerned with social development issues; the DSD acts as the secretariat for the CSocD)
Earth Summit	see UNCED

Earth Summit 2002 *see* WSSD
EC   European Commission
EC   European Community
ECA   UN Economic Commission for Africa
ECE   *see* UNECE
ECLAC   UN Economic Commission for Latin America and
                         the Caribbean
ECO   NGO newsletter brought out at a number of UN
                         events
ECOSOC   UN Economic and Social Council
EIT   economies in transition (predominately refers to
                         countries in Central and Eastern Europe)
ELCI   Environmental Liaison Centre International
ENB   *Earth Negotiations Bulletin*
EOSG   UN Executive Office of the Secretary-General
ESCAP   UN Economic and Social Commission for Asia
                         and the Pacific
ESCWA   UN Economic and Social Commission for Western
                         Asia
EU   European Union (works as a group at
                         international meetings, in addition to the actions
                         of the European member states present; EU
                         presidency rotates every six months)
FAO   Food and Agricultural Organization
FDI   foreign direct investment
FMSP   First Meeting of the States Parties
G7   Group of 7 (industrialized countries)
G8   Group of 8 (industrialized countries, including the
                         Russian Federation)
G15   country grouping of Algeria, Argentina, Brazil,
                         Egypt, India, Indonesia, Jamaica, Malaysia,
                         Mexico, Nigeria, Peru, Senegal, Venezuela,
                         Federal Republic of Yugoslavia and Zimbabwe
G77 and China   Group of 77 and China (the original group of the
                         so-called non-aligned states; this is, in effect, the
                         negotiating bloc of the member countries present
                         and seeks to harmonize the negotiating positions
                         of its 133 developing-country members)
GA   General Assembly (UN)
GATT   General Agreement on Tariffs and Trade
GEF   Global Environmental Facility (the World Bank,
                         the UNDP and the UNEP established the

	multibillion-dollar GEF in 1990 to fund environmental programmes, especially in the South and in EIT)
GNP	gross national product
GPA	Global Plan of Action
GRULAC	regional country grouping used within the UN and encompassing Latin America and the Caribbean
Habitat II	second UN Conference on Human Settlements (Istanbul, 1996), known as the City Summit
HCHR	UN High Commissioner for Human Rights
high-level segment	ministerial-level part of the meeting where the most significant issues are decided
HIPC	heavily indebted poor countries
HURPEC	Human Rights and Peace Campaign
IACSD	UN Inter-Agency Committee on Sustainable Development (closed down in 2001; but at time of publication there was discussion of reopening the committee)
IAEA	International Atomic Energy Agency
ICC	International Chamber of Commerce
ICFTU	International Confederation of Free Trade Unions
ICLEI	International Council for Local Environmental Initiatives
ICPD	International Conference on Population and Development
ICSU	International Council for Scientific Union
IDT	International Development Target
IFAP	International Federation of Agricultural Producers
IFF	Intergovernmental Forum on Forests
IFI	international financial institution
IISD	International Institute for Sustainable Development
ILO	International Labour Organization
IMF	International Monetary Fund
INC	Intergovernmental Negotiating Committee
INSTRAW	UN International Research and Training Institute for the Advancement of Women
inter-sessional	official between-sessions meeting of one of the commissions
IPF	Intergovernmental Panel on Forests
ISO	International Standards Organization

ITU	International Telecommunication Union
IULA	International Union of Local Authorities
JUSSCANNZ	Japan, the US, Switzerland, Canada, Australia, Norway and New Zealand (non-EU industrialized countries that meet as a group to discuss various issues)
LAIA	Latin American Integration Association
LDC	least developed country
MAI	Multilateral Agreement on Investment
Major Groups	term used in Agenda 21 to describe nine sectors of society fundamental to achieving sustainable development: women; children and youth; indigenous people; NGOs; local authorities; workers and trade unions; business and industry; scientific and technological communities; and farmers
MEA	Multilateral Environmental Agreement
member state	a nation that is a member of the UN
MOP	Meeting of the Parties
NGLS	UN Non-Governmental Liaison Service
NGO	non-governmental organization
North	popular term to describe developed industrialized countries
NRG4SD	Network for Regional Governments for Sustainable Development
OECD	Organisation for Economic Co-operation and Development
OPEC	Organization of the Petroleum Exporting Countries
plenary	a session of a meeting where all parties are present and where formal decisions are taken
PM	permanent member
POPs	persistent organic pollutants
PrepCom	UN Preparatory Committee (name given to meetings for preparation and negotiation prior to a summit)
regional groups	Africa; Asia; Central and Eastern Europe (CEE); Latin America and the Caribbean (GRULAC); and the Western Europe and Others Group (WEOG) (these five regional groups meet privately to discuss issues and to nominate bureau members and other officials)

Rio +5	five-year review of the Earth Summit *see also* UNGASS
SBC	Secretary of the Basel Convention
SBI	Subsidiary Body for Implementation
SBSTA	Subsidiary Body for Scientific and Technological Advice
SDIN	Sustainable Development Issues Network
SEE	South-Eastern European
SEEYC	South Eastern European Youth Council
side event	an open lunch-time or evening event in the margins of the official sessions, usually related to the issues being negotiated
SIDS	small island developing states (especially important in relation to the Barbados Plan of Action for SIDS)
South	popular term to describe developing countries
SWOT	strengths, weaknesses, opportunities and threats
UK	United Kingdom
UN	United Nations
UNAIDS	Joint UN Programme on HIV/AIDS
UNCA	UN Correspondents Association
UNCED	UN Conference on Environment and Development (Rio, 1992), *known as* the Earth Summit
UNCTAD	UN Conference on Trade and Development
UNDP	UN Development Programme
UNECE	UN Economic Commission for Europe
UNEP	UN Environment Programme
UNESCO	UN Educational, Scientific and Cultural Organization
UNFF	UN Forum on Forests
UNGASS	UN General Assembly Special Session (mostly refers to the 19th Special Session of the General Assembly – the five-year review of the Earth Summit, *known as* Rio +5)
UN-Habitat	United Nations Human Settlements Programme (*formerly* UN Centre for Human Settlements)
UNHCR	UN High Commissioner for Refugees
UNICEF	United Nations Children's Fund
UNIDO	UN Industrial Development Organization
UNITAR	UN Institute for Training and Research
US	United States
UTO	United Towns Organization

WACLAC	World Associations of Cities and Local Authorities Coordination
WBCSD	World Business Council for Sustainable Development
WEOG	Western Europe and Others Group (regional country grouping within the UN encompassing Western Europe and Others, such as the US and Canada
WFP	World Food Programme
WHO	World Health Organization
WICE	World Industry Council for the Environment
WIPO	World Intellectual Property Organization
WMO	World Meteorological Organization
working group	sub-group of the main meeting, tasked with drafting language for the final documents
WSSD	World Summit on Sustainable Development (Johannesburg, 2002), *known as* Earth Summit 2002
WTO	World Trade Organization
YFEU	Youth Forum of the European Union

Chapter 1

So Why Is This Important To My Organization?

Few will have the greatness to bend history; but each of us can work to change a small portion of events, and in the total of all those acts will be written the history of this generation... It is from numberless diverse acts of courage and belief that human history is thus shaped. Each time a person stands up for an ideal, or acts to improve the lot of others, or strikes out against injustice, they send forth a tiny ripple of hope, and crossing each other from a million different centres of energy and daring, those ripples build a current which can sweep down the mightiest walls of oppression and resistance.

(Senator Robert Kennedy, University of Cape Town, South Africa, 6 June 1966)

INTRODUCTION

Working at the 'global level' can have enormous benefits for organizations that want to set agendas, fast-track an issue or hold governments accountable to previous promises.

Let us start with an example. During the five-year review of the Earth Summit (Rio +5) in 1997, an issue not on the agenda – that of the proposed Organisation for Economic Co-operation and Development (OECD) Multilateral Agreement on Investment (MAI) – was brought up informally by non-governmental organizations (NGOs) with heads of state and governments. Many governments had not appreciated what the OECD was doing and what the implications might be for them. NGOs had previously tried to bring their opposition to this issue to national capitals without any success. The contacts at Rio +5 ensured that the issue was addressed at the highest level of government. The MAI was dead within five months of Rio +5.

United Nations (UN) conferences and summits, in particular, but also conventions, offer an enormous opportunity to build considerable press coverage for an issue. This, consequently, helps to raise awareness levels around the world and puts pressure on governments to do something. The importance of media coverage for these events cannot be emphasized enough.

The 1990s saw a series of global conferences and summits organized by the UN:

- World Summit for Children (New York, 1990);
- UN Conference on Environment and Development (Rio de Janeiro, 1992);
- Human Rights Summit (Vienna, 1993);
- International Conference on Population and Development (Cairo, 1994);
- World Summit for Social Development (Copenhagen, 1995);
- Fourth World Conference on Women (Beijing, 1995);
- World Food Summit (Rome, 1996); and
- Second UN Conference on Human Settlements (Istanbul, 1996).

Each of these resulted in its own set of declarations, plans of action and conventions (see Table 1.1). Chapter 4 reviews the differences between these terms and others to help the reader understand the varying emphasis that governments and others give to them. But perhaps it would be useful to understand that the difference, in general, is between soft law (for example, declarations and plans of action) and hard law (for example, conventions). Hard law means that a government can potentially be held accountable for the (in)action, while soft law is aspirational.

Combined, the UN conferences and summits have mapped out a social and economic framework by which the world might manage its affairs. Even as the 1990s saw the explosion of globalization, these imperfect, but important, agreements were mapping a moral and equitable path for all of us to follow.

It is worth noting that the Earth Summit in Rio led to the development of the largest number of legally binding Multilateral

Environmental Agreements (MEAs) of any intergovernmental process in history. These covered climate, biodiversity, fisheries, desertification, chemicals and persistent organic pollutants.

Taken collectively, the outcomes from the summits and conferences represented an attempt by the world to set new norms and standards by which human beings might interact with each other and other species on this small planet.

Parallel to this, we also saw a massive increase in NGO action around the policies and meetings of the new World Trade Organization (WTO), the World Bank and the International Monetary Fund (IMF). This included direct action related to the lack of access to the meetings, as well as interacting on the content of the meetings.

Each of the UN conferences and summits, with the exception of the World Summit for Children, has had its own five-year review conference. To date, only the Children's Summit and the Earth Summit have also had ten-year follow-up meetings. Recently, some governments have questioned whether five or even ten years is too soon for significant progress to be seen, and have suggested moving to 15-year cycles.

This explosion of international negotiations led to a new generation of people and organizations discovering the UN as a forum for international policy-making. Many of these organizations did not at first know how to fully utilize processes effectively to put pressure on their governments. As a result, a new generation of lobbyists was born who found ways of utilizing the corridors and coffee bars of the UN to move their organizations' policy goals forward.

The UN events mentioned above had tens of thousands of stakeholders in attendance. Governments, at times, worried about the number attending, thinking that all of them would be lobbying! The reality is that the number of individuals actively lobbying at a global meeting is relatively small, something we hope that this book will change. There are several reasons for this. People attending are there for a number of motives other than lobbying. These include sharing experiences, organizing partnerships or just learning how the intergovernmental process operates. These can all be very valid and important activities for their organizations, provided that this is why they were sent.

It is important to be clear on why one is attending an international meeting and what action is needed to achieve the identified aims. It is also important to recognize the difference between the position of your organization and your personal beliefs – and to understand which you are authorized to act upon.

Table 1.1 Global United Nations conferences and summits of the 1990s

Summit/ conference	Declaration	Plan of action	Convention	New UN body created
World Summit for Children *New York, 1990*	World Declaration on the Survival, Protection and Development of Children	Plan of Action for Implementing the World Declaration on the Survival, Protection and Development of Children during the 1990s	–	–
UN Conference on Environment and Development (UNCED or Earth Summit) *Rio de Janeiro, 1992*	(a) Rio Declaration on Environment and Development (b) Statement of Forest Principles	Agenda 21: Programme of Action for Sustainable Development – 40-chapter document that covers environmental, social, economic and political concerns	(a) Framework Convention on Climate Change (b) Convention on Biological Diversity (c) Convention to Combat Desertification* (ratified 1994) (d) Agreement on Conservation and Management of Straddling and Highly Migratory Fish Stocks* (e) Stockholm Convention on Persistent Organic Pollutants* (not yet come into force) (f) Rotterdam Convention on Prior Informed Consent Procedures for Certain Hazardous Chemicals and Pesticides in International Trade* (not yet come into force)	(a) A new functioning Commission of the UN Economic and Social Council was created: the Commission on Sustainable Development (b) For UN internal coordination, the Interagency Committee on Sustainable Development was created (c) To advise the UN Secretary-General, a high-level advisory board was set up

Human Rights Summit *Vienna, 1993*	The Vienna Declaration	—	—	Led to the appointment of the first High Commissioner for Human Rights
International Conference on Population and Development (ICPD) *Cairo, 1994*	—	Programme of Action Adopted at the ICPD	—	—
World Summit for Social Development *Copenhagen, 1995*	The Copenhagen Declaration on Social Development	Programme of Action of the World Summit for Social Development	—	—
Fourth World Conference on Women *Beijing, 1995*	The Beijing Declaration	Platform for Action Adopted by the Fourth World Conference on Women	—	—
World Food Summit *Rome, 1996*	Rome Declaration on World Food Security	World Food Summit Plan of Action	—	—
Second UN Conference on Human Settlements (Habitat II) *Istanbul, 1996*	Istanbul Declaration on Human Settlements	Habitat Agenda	—	—

Note: * negotiated after, but as a result of, UNCED
Source: adapted from Hemmati and Seliger (2001)

Often, many individuals attending a conference would like to lobby but, unfortunately, do not know how. Many of those who do know how do not have enough time to transfer their skills. Not enough has been done over the years to address this issue. New people are often left to fend for themselves and, therefore, tend not to be effective for the first couple of international meetings that they attend. This exacts an enormous cost from their organization.

This book aims to provide a first step. We hope that it helps you to make an effective start.

WHY ATTEND A UN COMMISSION, CONVENTION, CONFERENCE OR SUMMIT MEETING?

Participation in a UN event is not a substitute for working at local, national or regional levels on any issue. Rather, it is a very useful complement to the work done at other levels. It provides information on what your government is saying at the international level, as well as an important global forum for communicating the concerns of constituencies at home.

International meetings offer an opportunity to place national government policies in front of their peer group – that is, the governments of other countries. The review of previous government commitments or the development of new ones gives stakeholders an opportunity to highlight their government's failures and successes. It may be that certain governments have, indeed, implemented very positive policies. Highlighting these can have a positive impact on relationships with your own government and can provide a standard that challenges other governments to move forward. This process can also provide an opportunity to influence your government to agree to policies that it might not have wished to commit to domestically.

The UN processes offer the opportunity to maintain pressure on governments and intergovernmental organizations. They also provide a chance to strengthen the goals of your organization. One of the most exciting and useful things about UN meetings is the access that they potentially provide to heads of state, ministers and top civil servants. It is, in some ways, the equivalent of being allowed onto the floor of your parliament. A stakeholder can literally walk up to any country desk and talk to the relevant civil servant or minister...assuming that they can be found!

There are many reasons for attending a UN commission, convention, conference or summit. In this chapter we look at five reasons, in particular:

1 **Lobbying:** many people assume that everyone going to a UN event is interested in lobbying their government or other governments. This isn't true; in fact, a relatively small number of stakeholder groups actually lobby. On the other hand, stakeholders could have much greater impact if more participants engaged in, at least, some amount of lobbying during a given event.

2 **Learning:** learning how the international process works can be a first step to understanding how to use it effectively. This, in turn, leads to putting more effective pressure on your government to implement desired outcomes.

3 **Working with other stakeholders:** the intervals around a meeting allow stakeholders to spend time with colleagues, building a coalition on an issue that may or may not be on the agenda. This activity can be part of a longer-term campaign to bring an issue onto the agenda or to work with others on a future regional or global campaign.

4 **Exchanging information:** this helps to clarify issues, share ideas, circulate intelligence on the agenda for later debates, and develop contacts and trust, as well as sending international messages. Many people who attend UN events want to discuss what they have been doing or want to see what others are doing. This space offers a great opportunity for 'show and tell' in what is, basically, an ideas festival.

5 **Organizing events:** many stakeholders organize events in the margins of the meetings. These can influence the negotiations, highlight an issue or highlight (in)action by their governments. Do not organize your events when negotiations are taking place – government delegates will not come and you should be spending the time lobbying. Try to organize events during break periods. If possible, try to host a meeting involving government and stakeholders (for example, industry, trade unions and local government). This will help you to build contacts and may be more media worthy.

When your organization is deciding to become active at the inter-governmental level, there is a need for cost–benefit analysis. Budgets need to account for the cost of sending staff who are working at this level to the meeting, but also for preparatory time. If you are going to participate effectively in a meeting, preparation is more than just purchasing a plane ticket and finding accommodation.

Organizing a stakeholder–'officeholder' meeting

During these events, meetings can be organized by stakeholders with appropriate heads of state or ministers. A well-organized meeting with a head of state or minister can end up delivering a change in a government's position, either at the meeting or back home. To set up well-organized meetings, stakeholders should consider the following components:

- Select a capable stakeholder co-chair who will direct the questions.
- Agree among stakeholders, ahead of time, on a series of short, one- to two-minute questions. Have back-up questions or comments ready for each. The government liaison person for the meeting will usually have asked what are the issues being addressed. Give this information – the objective is not to catch a minister out but to move the issue(s) forward.
- Assign a specific person to ask each question.
- Agree on the order of questions and supply this to the government liaison person before the meeting; but agree that the stakeholder co-chair will have the flexibility to change the order if the conversation goes in a particular direction.
- Always try to be positive by first framing the issue or negotiating problem effectively, and then asking open-ended questions (for example, 'What is your government's policy on that?' 'What will your government's response/strategy be for dealing with that?'). The follow-up question can then be the challenging one (for example, 'Might that still leave the problem of…?' 'Couldn't it, in fact, be much more effective to…?').

Creating alliances

The UN meetings also offer the possibility of creating 'alliances' within and between stakeholder groups and governments. These can be powerful, both for lobbying and afterwards, during the most important phase: implementation.

Step 1

Develop a clear idea of your own objectives:

- What do you want?
- Why?

- What is your minimum negotiating position: what is absolutely essential and why?
- Why haven't you secured the objective to date (for example, because of government policy, personalities, resource issues, other factors or a mixture of the above)?

Knowing your own interests well is essential in negotiating effectively with others.

Step 2

Try to discuss and understand the perspectives of those with different views (not only the 'what', but the 'why'). Sometimes the information you get indicates possible ways forward. Occasionally it helps to clarify the best negotiating tactic.

Think about all of the actors in a process – other NGOs, delegates, businesses, trade unions, international organizations and the secretariat. Even if you can't speak directly with someone in a key position, you can piece together a lot about their position from an informed dialogue with your or their colleagues.

Keep a list of the key governments and what their positions are as the meeting starts, and what and how these positions change as you go along. This should help you to see what progress you have made in influencing them.

Step 3

Try to engage by focusing on who you can work with and within what limits. Being clear about the limits helps to avoid disappointment and frustration.

Box 1.1 Groundwork for creating alliances

In 1997, at the five-year review of the Earth Summit (Rio +5), Stakeholder Forum co-chaired a meeting of stakeholders with European environment and development ministers. The stakeholder team included Greenpeace, Friends of the Earth, the World Wildlife Fund, ANPED (the Northern Alliance for Sustainability), the Royal Society for the Protection of Birds and Severn Trent Water plc. It surprised the ministers considerably that a water company was sitting with NGOs and putting forward a joint position on water and poverty. This strengthened the position of NGOs and the European Union advocated this position in the negotiations.

Chapter 2

International Context

Business as usual, government as usual, and perhaps even protest as usual are not giving us the progress needed to achieve sustainable development. Let's see if we can't work together to find better paths forward.

(Paul Hohnen, former strategic director for Greenpeace)

PROGRESS IN INVOLVING STAKEHOLDERS

Over the past 13 years there has been an enormous rise in the involvement of stakeholders at the United Nations (UN).[1] It needs to be remembered that the UN is an intergovernmental body. As such, many governments and UN officials have, in the past, seen the involvement of non-governmental organizations (NGOs) – the UN calls all stakeholders NGOs – as only to be tolerated in the margins of meetings. The 1990s saw an enormous change because of many factors, including the changing role of the state, globalization and the collective impact of the many stakeholders attending the various summits.

The UN conferences and summits, starting with the UN Conference on Environment and Development (UNCED or Earth Summit) in Rio de Janeiro in 1992, recognized this change and responded by giving responsibility for some aspects of the delivery of the global agreements to bodies other than governments – to stakeholders.[2] As this occurred, stakeholders sought to have more say in this interaction. The Rio summit was also one of the first summits where stakeholders appeared on government delegations as advisers. Unheard of before, this allowed stakeholders into what were normally closed governmental meetings.

When set up in 1993, the UN Commission on Sustainable Development (CSD), which had evolved from Rio, began experimenting further with the involvement of stakeholders. This displeased some governments, who were active in the other UN functioning commissions. The first chair of the CSD was the Malaysian ambassador, Ismail Razali, who started by allowing stakeholder observation at most meetings. Later, chairs of the CSD actually allowed the participation of stakeholders in the meetings. Another development occurred in 1995 when the CSD introduced a 'stakeholder day', which focused upon their contribution to delivering Agenda 21.

In fact, the CSD mandate set up by the UN General Assembly stressed the importance of stakeholders. The CSD's mandate (Resolution 1993/207) is to monitor progress on the implementation of Agenda 21 and activities related to the integration of environmental and developmental goals by governments, NGOs, and other UN bodies. Specifically, the CSD's mandate is to:

- Monitor progress towards the target of 0.7 per cent gross national product (GNP) from developed countries for overseas development aid.
- Review the adequacy of financing and the transfer of technologies as outlined in Agenda 21.
- *Receive and analyse relevant information from competent NGOs in the context of Agenda 21 implementation.*
- *Enhance dialogue with NGOs, the independent sector and other entities outside of the UN system, within the UN framework.*
- *Provide recommendations to the UN General Assembly through the Economic and Social Council (ECOSOC).*

As can be seen, the last three of these mandates (indicated by italics) relate to the responsibilities of stakeholders, as well as governments.

The Habitat II conference in 1996 (Second UN Conference on Human Settlements) also made significant breakthroughs in stakeholder involvement. The conference was also known as the City Summit; in particular, it recognized the role of local authorities in delivering the agreements negotiated. The UN does not recognize local authorities as governments, but as NGOs. One of the reasons for this is that opposition parties run many local authorities; therefore, governments are uneasy about their involvement, other than as part of a global association of local authorities.

The innovation at Habitat in involving stakeholders also resulted in a different structure to the conference. The conference consisted of two committees. Committee 1 dealt with negotiating the outstanding paragraphs in the Istanbul Declaration and the Habitat II Agenda. Committee 2 was a series of half-day dialogues with each stakeholder group presenting their thoughts on what they believed were key to the Habitat Agenda, and then entering into dialogue with governments and other stakeholders. The reality was that, since the negotiations were going on in committee 1, the level of participation in the dialogues by government officials was low and the input from these to the negotiations was zero. However, in retrospect, it was hugely significant as it began what would evolve to be a whole new approach to stakeholder involvement.

The idea of these dialogues was promoted by NGOs that had been active in Habitat II, and later adopted by the UN General Assembly (GA) in October 1996. The GA was discussing the framework for the 19th GA Special Session (UNGASS) in 1997 to review implementation of the Earth Summit outcomes. The idea presented to the General Assembly was that each major group (stakeholder group) would be asked to report at the Second Preparatory Committee (PrepCom 2) what it had achieved in implementing Agenda 21. The General Assembly agreed to this in November 1996 and asked each of the stakeholders to prepare for half-day dialogue sessions. Again, one of the problems was that these were held while the negotiations were happening. As a result, governments sent low-level representation, if any at all. Nevertheless, the idea of holding stakeholder dialogues at future CSD meetings was agreed and was written into the CSD's next five-year work programme. Another advancement at UNGASS was the recognition given to the nine stakeholder groups, who for the first time ever were each given a slot to address the heads of state section of the meeting.

In 1998, the agreed topic for the dialogues was 'industry'. The then director of the UN Division on Sustainable Development, Joke Waller Hunter, brought together the International Chamber of Commerce and the World Business Council on Sustainable Development, the International Confederation of Free Trade Unions and the CSD NGO Steering Committee. Under her leadership, a new formula was agreed. This included the breakthrough that the negotiations would not take place parallel to the dialogues but would occupy the first two days of the CSD. The first dialogue had three major stakeholder groups participating: industry, trade unions and NGOs. Each stakeholder group consulted and produced a starting paper on the sub-themes of:

- responsible entrepreneurship;
- corporate management tools;
- technology cooperation and assessment; and
- industry and freshwater.

These papers were distributed as UN background papers before the CSD inter-sessional in March that year so that governments would have time to reflect on them as they discussed each issue for the first time. One of the more important by-products of this approach was that it caused 'peer group' review within each of the stakeholder groups. Most of the stakeholders worked on a four-level preparation:

1 Two people, usually one from a developed country and one from a developing country, devised an initial draft.
2 The stakeholder group coordinator – usually a staff person with the stakeholder coordination body – liaised with those interested in reviewing the paper. These reviewers had a gender and regional balance.
3 The paper was circulated to those members of the stakeholder group with interest in that particular issue. A time limit was set for feedback to be submitted.
4 The original authors revised the paper and, time permitting, it went out for a further round of consultation.

Another important outcome was that comments that could previously only be made to governments in the corridors could now be made in a 'creative' forum, where reasons for and against were given and challenged, all as a part of the official process. Some governments enjoyed this role reversal and the opportunity of being able to put stakeholder groups under the microscope regarding their position. However, some governments were unhappy with the idea that they had to listen to stakeholder groups and saw this as an encroachment on governmental negotiating space.

The eventual success of the dialogues was, in part, due to the successive CSD chairs, starting with the then Philippine minister of the environment, Cielito Habito. He challenged the stakeholder groups on their positions and led the sessions to become a very vibrant exchange between, and among, stakeholder groups and governments. This led to the birth of the first really dynamic model for stakeholder engagement in an ongoing UN process.

The outcome from the 1998 dialogues was the setting up of a multi-stakeholder review of voluntary initiatives. Sadly, the follow-up did not deliver the quality that had been expected from the suggestion. There were many reasons for this; but the critical one was that there were no funds committed to facilitate a review other than a workshop in Canada. For the review to be successful, reasonable financial support was needed for the three stakeholder groups participating, as well as for the initiative's secretariat.

In 1999 the dialogues addressed tourism. In order to ensure a better focus, the CSD NGO Steering Committee, an international coalitionof NGOs, suggested that the stakeholder-generated papers should not exceed four pages and should adopt the following structure:

- problems;
- solutions;
- institutional responsibilities; and
- possible partnerships.

The active involvement during the preparatory process of the 1999 CSD Chair Simon Upton, then New Zealand minister for the environment, played a critical role in another successful dialogue. Through his office a meeting was convened in London by David Taylor of the New Zealand government, where representatives of all the stakeholder groups were brought together at the CSD to identify their level of agreement and disagreement. This helped to focus the dialogues and increase the areas of agreement.

The other significant breakthrough that Simon Upton achieved was issuing the outcomes from the dialogues as a letter to governments at the beginning of the second week of the CSD, which enabled outcomes to be drawn into the negotiations. It is unfortunate that this approach has not since been taken during the following years, as the dialogues' outcomes have not been easily brought into the negotiations.

The outcomes of the CSD dialogue sessions have been important in setting up ongoing multi-stakeholder work. They have also helped to build trust between stakeholder groups. In all, there has been an enormous leap in stakeholder group involvement in the UN. Instead of the work and expertise of the stakeholder groups being part of a side show, or being confined to the corridors, they are now being incorporated within preparations for the negotiations – helping governments to take better-informed positions.

The idea of dialogues has started to appear in other UN processes, such as the Forum on Forests, Financing for Development and the UN Environment Programme (UNEP) Governing Council, as well as in meetings of the Food and Agricultural Organization (FAO) and ECOSOC. A problem however is that different UN bodies are using the term 'dialogue' to mean different things. Therefore, stakeholders coming into a space are often confused about what is expected of them. During 2001, Stakeholder Forum made significant attempts to try to create some norms and standards by looking at approximately 20 dialogue processes around the globe and producing a guide on how best to approach stakeholder engagement.[3]

During 2001, the German government organized a multi-stakeholder dialogue with ministers for the Bonn Freshwater Conference. The model developed at Bonn proved very effective, although most of its successes have yet to be adopted by the UN. Some of the significant advances from Bonn are:

- In addition to stakeholder groups developing their own positions, preparations between stakeholder groups encouraged them to identify what they might agree on.
- Areas of focus and disagreement were addressed by bringing together stakeholders in a facilitated pre-meeting.
- A facilitator was introduced to guide the dialogues.
- Half of the dialogue time was allocated to governments.
- A strict two-minute time limit for contributions was introduced by the facilitator.
- Only one or two aspects of an issue were focused upon.
- The outcomes from the dialogues were brought into the formal negotiation process.

The World Summit on Sustainable Development (WSSD or Earth Summit 2002) in Johannesburg was the ten-year review of UNCED. Stakeholder dialogues were held at the Regional Preparatory Committee Meetings (PrepComs),[4] two at the second and fourth PrepComs and at the summit itself. Many viewed these dialogues as a setback since there was no link with the official decision-making process, and the topics did not help governments to reach better-informed decisions.

Stakeholder dialogues, as a form of helping governments to make better decisions, are here to stay. The design of them is critical for everyone to feel that their work is valued and for effective contributions to be made.

In 1992, the Earth Summit established that governments alone could not deliver the global agreements; Agenda 21 identified nine other stakeholders who also had responsibilities. The five-year review

(Rio +5) introduced multi-stakeholder dialogues to help governments make better-informed decisions. The WSSD added that stakeholders working together could have a big impact in implementation.

Since stakeholders, individually, are already involved in delivering sustainability, it will be interesting if in 2012, the ten-year review of the WSSD is also reviewing the delivery of stakeholder partnerships for sustainable development against the Millennium Declaration goals.

Chapter 3

Preparation

Vision without action is merely a dream.
Action without vision just passes the time.
Vision with action can change the world!
(Joel Arthur Barker, president of Infinity Limited)

TOOLS TO PREPARE: SCENARIO-BUILDING AND SWOT ANALYSES

Once your organization has decided what it wants to achieve, the challenge becomes figuring out a political strategy to accomplish it.

Scenario-building

Scenario-building and analysis can be a very useful tool that helps politically to:

- understand how a situation may evolve; and
- develop strategies to influence it.

There are many different types of scenario analysis; which one you use will depend upon what you want to do. Developmental scenarios tell a story. Future histories tell the same story backwards. End-state scenarios describe the future you want without necessarily outlining how to get there. A morphological approach breaks the problem down into its component sub-systems, brainstorms the alternative states each sub-system could take and then systematically combines the results to create a range of scenarios. There are other methods. No matter which method you choose, the objective is not to predict the future but to understand the range of behaviours that the system may exhibit and develop strategies to cope with that range.

About a year before the World Summit on Sustainable Development (WSSD) a number of NGOs convened a small meeting that used the 'matrix method' to develop scenarios to explore the range of potential outcomes of the summit. This information was then used to develop lobbying strategies to influence the preparatory process of the summit.

The meeting profiled the major stakeholders in the summit process. Who was influential? What outcomes did they hope for from the summit? What was their bottom line? The NGOs recorded this information in a 'stakeholder matrix'. As they talked, they started to get a feel for the various dynamics that might play out in the summit. They then used this information to prepare scenarios using the matrix method.

In the matrix method, there are two axes or dimensions that describe or structure the space that is to be explored. Finding the right axis for the matrix is crucial to success. It is largely an inductive process that benefits from a clear understanding of the system. Once the axes are identified, it is a deductive process to fill in the details in each box (scenario) within the matrix.

From the stakeholder analysis, the NGOs realized that the two important variables that would shape the whole summit were:

1   the degree of political will (high or low); and
2   the state of the global economy (growth or recession).

They used these two variables to create the matrix (see Figure 3.1). There are four cells within the matrix. Each cell represents one scenario. For instance, in the upper left-hand corner, the scenario is defined by 'high political will' and 'strong economic growth'. They used the information from the stakeholder analysis to anticipate how the stakeholders would behave under these circumstances and then to deduce an overall outcome, which was summarized as 'New Deal'.

Between the GA decision to hold the summit and the summit itself, the world went through massive political changes: the September 11 terrorist attacks in the US and subsequent repercussions; and changes in governments in three critical nations – the US, The Netherlands and Denmark (holder of the European Union (EU) presidency during the WSSD).

Figure 3.1 *Scenario-building for WSSD: The Matrix Method*

In developing NGOs' strategy, it was clear that the US would be a critical player whatever party was in power. There were two possible approaches that could be applied to the US. One was to isolate it and the other was to work as closely as possible with it. To isolate the US would require the EU to take a formidable leadership role, and – with the balance within Europe moving from left to right – it was unlikely that the Europeans would be able to undertake this leadership role in all areas. The EU's ability to influence negotiations is limited by two factors:

1   The presidency undertakes nearly all of the negotiations and lobbying. This means that the other countries' officials are not utilized properly.
2   The coordination meetings of the EU take the key European negotiators out of the corridors (a situation that will get worse after enlargement).

This would leave the corridors free much of the time, and it was clear that the US would be populating this space with a formidable team, both in quality and quantity. It was therefore critical for some stakeholders to retain a good relationship with the US team of negotiators. Although the political people had changed or were changing throughout the summit process, working closely with the US to try to help move forward areas that might be flexible was critical for delivering the New Deal scenario.[1]

As 2001 rolled out, it became clear that there would not be a strong economy; therefore, the possibility of a New Deal started to diminish.

In retrospect, the scenarios where both useful for strategy development and somewhat prescient. The actual outcome of the summit could be summerized as 'sustainable development delayed'. Global economic uncertainty combined with moderate political will keep sustainable development alive; but implementation still lies in the future.

Groups preparing for lobbying too often overlook the larger political context. It helps to focus efforts in the context of larger dynamics and also helps to take a realistic account of the resources at hand. A simple starting point may be creating a table of the event's key players and looking at their present position, likely position and bottom line.

SWOT analysis

SWOT stands for strengths, weaknesses, opportunities and threats. A SWOT analysis is often the first step in a formal strategic planning exercise. There is much written on this method; but, essentially, it is a relatively simple tool that can aid lobbying efforts (see Box 3.1). It can be applied at both the organizational level of a campaign, as well as at the policy or idea level. This kind of analysis can help an organization address its weaknesses and threats, while maximizing its strengths and opportunities. The main benefit is that it helps to identify mistaken assumptions and then to re-organize or re-conceptualize for greater impact.

It can also be useful to engage other stakeholders (including governments) in a SWOT analysis in order to better understand where they are coming from and their constraints.

NATIONAL PREPARATIONS

If you are going to attend a UN meeting, then you should try to ensure that you have been active nationally before you go. This would include the following.

Lobbying your government

It is important that before you attend any UN meeting, you should undertake proper preparation: contact your government and make it

Box 3.1 Elements and questions for a SWOT analysis

1 SWOT – strengths

- What is the unique nature of the campaign?
- What does the team do well?
- What do other people see as your strengths?

When answering these questions, write them from both your perspective and other key players' perspectives.

2 SWOT – weaknesses

- What can you improve?
- What are your resource limitations?
- What do you do badly?
- How do others perceive your campaign?
- Do you know what all the key governments think of your campaign?

This should again be viewed both internally and externally.

3 SWOT – opportunities

- Where is the campaign's support?
- What academic evidence is there in support of your campaign?
- What are the key media opportunities you could utilize to support your campaign?
- Who is seeing key government officials in the short term?

4 SWOT – threats

- What are the obstacles facing the campaign?
- What funds do you have to support the campaign?
- What are the views of other stakeholders?
- Which of the key country blocs oppose your campaign?

clear what issues you want them to raise. They may agree with your position, in which case you should work with them to put pressure on other governments when you attend the UN meeting.

If they disagree, then you will need to start a dialogue to change their view. It is important to know on what basis they are taking that view. Is it government policy or is it in the area of civil service decision-making? You may want to utilize your national legislature (for example, parliament) to put pressure on government regarding specific positions that they are taking. This needs to be done well in advance of the UN meeting.

Most governments work in blocs – for example, the EU and the Group of 77 developing countries (G77) – and will have to go through a consultation process within the group to come to a common position. This can start up to four months before a meeting.

One of the first things that you need to find out from your government are the timelines within which it is working so that you can input at the right moment. Too often, stakeholders prepare the weekend before a UN meeting and then, at the end of the meeting, wonder why they have not been very successful.

Identifying officials

It is very important to understand that there is a difference between civil servants and elected government ministers or political appointees. In international negotiations, there are often grey areas, and officials, particularly for countries with small delegations, can do a lot in drafting particular policies. Many delegations have one or two staff covering a number of UN commissions and are happy for extra help. You can be an enormous help to them in drafting text and giving advice. If you can identify understaffed delegations early enough, it could be very useful to bring into the meeting a stakeholder representative from that country.

If this is the first time that you have approached an official, it is important that you try to do it well before a meeting. Send a letter, introducing yourself and your organization, in addition to information that is relevant to the meeting coming up, and say that you will be calling soon to have an informal chat.

If you disagree with the political party in power, do not treat officials as if they are a member of that party. They may not be. It is very important to meet the officials and get to know them in a friendly atmosphere. This can be done through official meetings where you are with other stakeholders asking the government to explain its policies. However, it should also be done informally well before the meeting, perhaps over a coffee and away from the government offices, where you can have more informal discussions.

You should also request a meeting with the minister before crucial international meetings so that she or he can hear directly what the views are of different stakeholders. It may be that the minister will be prepared to compromise or change the government's views, or that the views are not held by the ministry that you are lobbying. A strong message from a number of groups may help that ministry in inter-departmental discussions to change the views of others. It is vital that you identify the government's roadblock to any change of policy and focus your work there. If the problem is in another ministry, then you need to focus your energy on that ministry. If it is a summit process and the head of state is going, then there will be people in that office coordinating what he or she is going to say. It is important to find out who the aides are early on and to organize meetings with them as well. They will be announcing initiatives and will also be in charge of the head of state's speech. If you have ideas on initiatives, then your input has to be early enough for it to go through intergovernmental departmental processes. Governments will normally set up an ad-hoc interdepartmental committee for an important UN event.

Working with others

For a UN meeting, it is likely that many stakeholders will be attending and your organization should link with any preparatory work being conducted in your country. Your organization should also find out what meetings are being planned on the issues in which you are interested. If you can agree on joint positions within a stakeholder group, or even between stakeholder groups, then governments are more likely to take notice. The broader the basis of any coalition, the more likely it is that a government will listen to the views expressed.

National reports

For many UN meetings, governments are requested to produce a national report. This report reviews progress made in implementing past agreements that it has signed up to. This offers a great opportunity for groups if a dialogue with their government is started early enough. The design of the review document may be pre-set by the UN, but is likely to be very flexible. The kind of timelines used by the UN for a meeting at the beginning of March would require a national report to be sent in to the relevant UN official by the beginning of the previous October to enable them to synthesize all of the national reports into a UN Secretary-General report, which would then be released not later than six weeks before the meeting.

With this timeline in mind, a discussion with your government on how it is going to compile the report, and what input it would like from stakeholders, can be very productive. The government, in many cases, will have to consult several government departments about what they have or have not done. However, many UN agreements are not only about government action, but about action by others. Governments generally do not like to show that they haven't done something required of them; so how stakeholders address this can be critical to the relationship. Focusing on successes and roadblocks gives an opportunity for a balanced approach. If you can persuade the relevant government department to look at the roadblocks, it may help them with their interdepartmental discussions.[2]

One of the objectives for stakeholders participating in creating a national report is to enable the information required for future implementation to be made available. The opportunity that such a review offers is not just to look back at what has or has not been done, but, in many cases, to look at issues for the first time. A proper national report process may set in motion work that should have been done before but has not.

A two-way dialogue is usually the best objective. Even if a non-governmental organization (NGO) seeks something that the government is unlikely to be able to support, developing a good working relationship will produce a better climate for movement in the future. It also means that there is more likely to be a reasonable discussion of issues. No one wants to be frozen out – either at home or in an international meeting – because they have then completely lost the ability to communicate on an issue. Remember that government negotiators are talking about stakeholders in just the same way as stakeholders talk about which government negotiators can be worked with or not!

Dealing with the media

At least two weeks before you leave for a UN meeting you should prepare a background briefing for the press on what is likely to happen. This may persuade them to attend the meeting or to write a preliminary story. At the very least, it will enable them to understand what the meeting is all about. You should also hold a debriefing the week you get back on the outcomes and possible implementation implications for your country.

Before you leave for the UN meeting, arrange for a group of staff or other stakeholders to be available to take action in your country's capital when the UN meeting is in progress. This may involve dealing with the media, with parliament or with the minister, if they are not at the meeting. For example, in one environmental negotiation, a US official took a position that was not in keeping with the position of the

Clinton administration. A US NGO reported this to the minister and the position was changed very quickly. But this type of action should be a last resort, as the official will remember your actions and it will make your relationship much more difficult in future. It may also be that having people available at home enables conversations with the media who are not attending the meeting but who could help to create pressure in the capital on problem issues at the UN meetings.

Remember to take the email and telephone details of your key press contacts with you to UN meetings.

GLOBAL PREPARATIONS

Why work at the global level at all? This is a question that many of us who have been working in the area ask at times. The inter-governmental bodies, such as the UN and the World Trade Organization (WTO), set the international rules by which the world tries to operate, whether it's sending a letter, making a telephone call, determining how we maintain our environment, how we trade, or how we deal with security issues. These bodies are only ever able to do what governments permit them to do or wish them to do. In many cases, it comes down to the relinquishing by governments of their national sovereignty.

During the 1990s, the UN conferences and summits on sustainable development, women, human rights, population, social development and human settlements developed a large amount of soft law in the area of human interaction with the planet and with each other. The follow-up to these conferences and summits has been through the functioning commissions of the UN Economic and Social Council (ECOSOC),[3] which are the:

- Commission on Sustainable Development (CSD);
- Commission on the Status of Women;
- Commission on Human Rights;
- Commission on Population and Development;
- Commission for Social Development (CSocD).

The rules of stakeholder engagement in these commissions are set by the UN Committee on Non-Governmental Organizations, which has a membership of 19 countries, elected through its regional groupings. It sets a standard governing what NGOs (stakeholders) can do with the ECOSOC and its subsidiary bodies. More progressive commissions, such as the CSD, have developed the involvement of NGOs beyond the rules laid down by the committee.

Governments

The negotiating body for a UN meeting made up of governments. The number and distribution of governments depends upon the meeting. If it is a summit or conference, then all UN member states are entitled to participate. If it is a convention, then those who have ratified are entitled. For a UN commission, it will be either the number of countries identified in the UN General Assembly resolution setting up the commission or as outlined in a subsequent UN General Assembly resolution. At present, it ranges between 40 and 54 countries who are elected through their regional blocs. For many meetings, the negotiators will be from the foreign ministries – usually representatives at the countries' Permanent Mission to the UN – supported by delegations from relevant ministries from the capitals. For some of the smaller countries, the delegation will be made up entirely of UN Mission representatives.

Key governments or blocs to be aware of include the following.

The European Union

The EU is, at present, made up of 15 countries.[4] It operates with each of the countries undertaking the presidency for a six-monthly rotational period. These are from January to the end of June and from July to the end of December. They also operate a Troika, which guides a presidency and is made up of the previous presidency, the current presidency and the succeeding presidency. Find out in the current presidency country who the relevant civil servant is who deals with your issue.

The role and duties of the EU presidency involve the:

- management and enhancement of cooperation between EU members in the European Council, the Council of Ministers and the Committee of Permanent Representatives (COREPER);
- representation of the Council of the European Union in other EU institutions and organs (especially the European Parliament and the European Commission); and
- representation of the EU in international organizations, meetings and fora, and in its relations with developing countries.

The further one moves into the negotiations, the more difficult it is to get the EU to accept new ideas, persuading 15 countries (25 in 2004) that the issue is worth consideration, and obviously this is more difficult as the text moves to bracketing. When countries cannot agree, they will bracket text. The more text without bracketing, the more agreement exists (for further explanation of brackets, see the section 'The World of Brackets'). The only EU country that will usually talk in the negotiations will be the presidency. European coordination for a meeting will start at least six months before the meeting, and the EU may have assigned different governments to develop the initial position paper for its discussion on an issue. It is very important to know which government is doing the initial papers and to contact it at the very beginning. If possible, go and see the relevant civil servant in their capital. If you do this, it is useful to have a national counterpart to facilitate the meeting.

The European Commission staff play a key role behind the scene, particularly in areas where the commission has competence – for example, agriculture. Developing a good relationship with them and visiting to discuss issues as they are developing their first papers is always productive.

Most European countries and the European Commission itself will have stakeholders on their government and commission delegations. Those on government delegations may be allowed to attend European coordination meetings. These allow you to identify who the key countries are that agree with your views and who the key ones are that do not. It also allows you 'informal time' with the officials from all of the governments, not just the one you are on the delegation with. Invite key government representatives out for drinks or coffee. Identify who will take the presidency at the UN meeting and build your relationship there.

Summary

- Know the European timelines.
- Know which country is drafting the discussion paper on each issue.
- Create a relationship with the relevant EU presidency civil servants.
- Know the relevant European staff.
- Seek to become a stakeholder representative on the delegation.

The Group of 77 and China

The Group of 77 (G77) was established on 15 June 1964 by 77 developing countries, all signatories of the Joint Declaration of the 77 Countries issued at the end of the first session of the UN Conference on Trade and Development (UNCTAD) in Geneva. The chair of the G77 rotated through the relevant UN regions: Africa, Asia, Latin America and the Caribbean, and West Asia. The position is held for a year; but recently the G77 has been developing its own Troika approach involving the previous chair, the current chair and the forthcoming chair. The Organization of the Petroleum Exporting Countries (OPEC) group has had an increasing impact on who chairs the G77. From 2000 to 2002, the chair was an OPEC member country.

Although the membership of the G77 has increased to 133 countries, it retained its original name because of its historic significance. The G77 has a formidable task with so many countries to coordinate and with very diverse economies and interests. Within the G77 there are many interest groups depending upon the issue being discussed. In some cases, regional or interest groups may make separate statements – for example, the Alliance of Small Island States (AOSIS), which has 42 members and observers. Although the G77 is large, certain countries tend to take a leading role (Brazil, China, Egypt, Iran, India, Indonesia, Malaysia, Nigeria, Pakistan, Saudi Arabia, South Africa and Venezuela). Some countries within G77 will also take stakeholders on their delegation. This allows stakeholders to identify which are the key countries to be targeted. For example, it may be that in a particular process, only 20 to 30 of the G77 governments are major players. China does not always associate with the G77, and in those cases the chair of the G77 will only speak for the others.

The chairs of the G77 since the UN conferences and summits started during the 1990s have been Bolivia, Ghana, Colombia, Algeria, the Philippines, Costa Rica, Tanzania, Indonesia, Guyana, Nigeria, Iran, Venezuela and Morocco. Unlike the EU, there is no staff support for the G77 chair other than that given by the country that is chairing. This places the G77 at a considerable political disadvantage.

Summary

- Know the G77 timelines.
- Know which country in the G77 is leading for a particular issue.
- Create a relationship with the relevant country official(s).
- Create a relationship with some staff within the G77 chair's office.

JUSSCANNZ

The non-EU industrialized countries meet as a group to discuss various issues. These are Japan, the US, Switzerland, Canada, Australia, Norway and New Zealand. Iceland, Mexico and the Republic of South

Korea may also attend meetings. This bloc does not often work as a formal negotiating group – more as an ad-hoc group. If it does work together, than this tends to be with considerable US pressure and will be a conservative force within the negotiations. It is not usually in the interest of stakeholders for this group to work together as it includes countries which can be lobbied to take individual positions.

Bureau

Governments will elect a bureau, which will be based on one or two countries from each of the UN regions, to manage the preparations and the meeting itself. Bureau members tend to be representatives from UN missions to the relevant UN centre – for example, New York, Geneva and Vienna. Some UN meetings will utilize officials from capitals – for example, the Commission on Sustainable Development Bureau will usually be chaired by a sitting or former minister.

The bureau plays a critical role in managing the process. It can guide the direction of the negotiations through the structuring of the text and the inclusion, in first drafts, of certain ideas. Bureau members are in touch with thinking in the different groups, and discussing ideas with them can, particularly at the beginning of a process, be an informal way of having your views expressed to others without having to do it yourself. You should find out who the bureau members are and meet with them well before the relevant meeting. It is well worth an early visit to New York eight to ten weeks before the UN meeting to meet bureau members and key government representatives in the UN missions and the UN Secretariat. The positions that you have are worth sharing with bureau members if they are sympathetic to your views.

Permanent members (PMs) of the UN Security Council are not allowed to be bureau members, although some PMs do sneak in through chairing preparatory meetings. They can then be found as ex-officio members of the bureau. During the first ten years of the UN Commission on Sustainable Development, the UK managed this three times!

The Secretariat

In every UN process, there is a Secretariat that plays a critical role. This includes:

- preparing the background documents;
- producing or updating a website for the meeting;

- analysing the national reports;
- producing promotional material for the meeting;
- producing negotiating text arising from the discussions;
- making available all official documents;
- servicing the negotiations; and
- accrediting stakeholders.

The secretariat can play a very important role in drafting the original text upon which governments then deliberate. There can be a tendency in secretariats, generally, for the first text handed to governments to be too bland and middle of the road. If governments start negotiating this, then the outcome is likely to be poor. In the Habitat II process the secretariat text was rejected at the end of two of the UN Preparatory Meetings, and in each case the negotiators had to begin again. A strong political bureau can, in these instances, be very important. If the bureau takes control of some of the drafting, then it can often be closer to its colleagues than the UN Secretariat. An activist bureau is more likely if there is a political chair – for example, a minister as opposed to a civil servant. Ministers are more likely to focus on clear outcomes.

It is very important to discover the author of the original background paper from which the negotiations will start. These papers are issued as UN Secretary-General papers. Create a relationship with the author, who will be analysing material from a number of sources, such as government reports, UN agency and programme inputs and also input from stakeholders. The timelines on this are very early – the author can start collecting input up to nine months before the relevant meeting at which the paper will be delivered. The paper will usually be finished around four months before the meeting to allow for the review process inside the UN and for time to translate the paper into the UN official languages. It will be released six weeks before the meeting to enable governments to consult in capitals.

Building relationships with the authors of the original text can pay very good dividends. In one UN summit negotiation, a part of the text had not been negotiated in any of the PrepComs. NGOs gave their text suggestions directly to the relevant UN official, who put them all in the next draft that came out.

UN agencies, programmes and funds

In many processes the original UN Secretary-General's paper(s) will be produced by the most relevant UN agency – for example, for Agenda 21, the UN Educational, Scientific and Cultural Organization (UNESCO) produced the paper on education. In other areas, UN staff with the commission might write the paper – for example, the Division for the Advancement of Women as the secretariat to the Commission on the Status of Women.

UN agencies and programmes are very important as they usually have field or intellectual understanding of the key issues that you will address. Sometimes rivalry between them can cause problems in a negotiation.

Major Groups/Stakeholders

The 1990s saw an enormous increase in the number of NGOs that were accredited to the UN and active in conference processes. In 1946, there were only four NGOs accredited. By 1992, this had grown to 928 and by the end of 2000 this had increased to 2091. Table 3.1 reviews the number of ECOSOC-recognized NGOs before and after each review of consultative status.

The rules that govern NGOs' involvement within ECOSOC are based on a 1996 ECOSOC resolution.

Starting with the Earth Summit in Rio in 1992 and followed by the conferences on human rights, population, social development, women, human settlements and food there was a large influx of NGOs. They also brought a new generation of organizations and individuals to the UN, who saw it as a vehicle to highlight their concerns and a place to put pressure on their own, as well as other, governments.

Table 3.1 *Number of ECOSOC-recognized NGOs before and after each review of consultative status*

Year	Category A [1/General status]	Category B [2/Special status]	Register [Roster]	Total
1946	4	0	0	4
1949	9	77	4	90
1950	9	78	110	197
1968	12	143	222	377
1969	16	116	245	377
1992	41	354	533	928
1996	80	500	646	1226
1998	103	745	671	1519

Source: Willetts (1999, p250)

Stakeholders on delegation

As mentioned previously, some governments include stakeholders on their delegations for meetings within the sphere of ECOSOC. A few (for example, Norway and the UK) have even had NGOs on their delegation to the UN General Assembly. Being on the government delegation usually means that you are there to give advice on a particular issue or to act as a link between the government and the other stakeholders attending the meeting. In delegation meetings, you would be expected to put forward these stakeholder views and not just your own. Some stakeholders are intimidated by government coordination meetings and find it difficult to contribute as they may feel like an outsider. Just because the government has agreed to you being on delegation does not mean that the civil servants feel relaxed about it. If you haven't met with them over the previous few months to talk about the issues, then you may find it difficult to contribute or for your views to be taken seriously.

The best time to go on delegation is six months before the meeting. If you can persuade your government, you should be present as they develop their views. If they are prepared to treat you as part of the team, then attending all of their main internal preparatory meetings will give you a key understanding of how they are taking outside views into consideration, but also how they are dealing with interdepartmental pressure. It is unlikely that they will be prepared to give you this kind of access to the internal governmental machinery; but even a slimmed-down version of this is worth fighting for. What you are suggesting isn't just a one-way advantage for you – they will benefit enormously from your advice on, and appreciation of, how issues will play out.

The usual way of governments to involve those stakeholders on delegation is to have only one meeting before departing for the UN event, and then invite them to the preparatory meeting the day before the UN meeting occurs, as well as to subsequent daily meetings. Obviously, this is not ideal, either for the stakeholders or the delegation overall.

All governments work with a government brief that has been prepared for the meeting. This contains the position of the government and outlines what can be conceded in negotiations and what cannot. Beyond the brief, officials have to go back to the capital to ask for new instructions. If you are joining a delegation, in order for you to be effective, you need a copy of this document. Some governments are worried that stakeholders on delegations will leak the brief and are reluctant to allow them to see it. Some stakeholders have, in the past, leaked briefs. A certain amount of diplomacy is required. To not release documents can be viewed as 'selling out' by colleagues. Do not compromise the opportunity for others to be invited on delegations in the future. Remember that stakeholders are on delegations in many of the social and economic fields, and irresponsible action in one area can seriously impact upon others. If you feel at any point that working inside the delegation is a conflict, then resign. If you find out something that would not be discovered through normal corridor work, but which would seriously impact upon the negotiations – and you feel that you cannot continue as a member of the delegation because of this position – then resign.

If you have been on a government delegation a number of times, they will trust you more than if it is your first time. Some governments require you to sign a form of non-disclosure of information, and this usually also lists what you cannot do in other areas, as well. If you are not sure, ask the head of delegation.

While you are on the delegation, you need to accept the discipline not to release the brief no matter how tempting it might be. If you do, then the result could be:

- You are taken off delegation – this might mean that you are unable to attend the UN meeting as you have lost your accreditation to the meeting.
- You may have ensured that any future stakeholder on the delegation does not see the brief.
- You will have created serious problems for all of the other stakeholders attending the meeting, as the officials will pull back from sharing with them.
- It could compromise future credibility for having stakeholders on delegation.

Innovations

There have been many innovations that stakeholders have made to improve their ability to be effective at UN meetings. The following sections list a few that might be helpful.

Delegates' photos

Stakeholder Forum operates a relatively unique approach to preparing for a meeting. In addition to training for staff and others, it gives its team members a photographic delegate display of key officials. This helps new members start lobbying from day one. For the WSSD process, the photos were extracted from the *Earth Negotiations Bulletin* website (www.iisd.ca),[5] which features a set of photographs of all of the key government, UN and stakeholder representatives. These photographs, of course, make it much easier to identify officials to whom you need to speak. The photos can then be updated as the negotiations move forward and new people start taking key roles.

Floor managers

If your stakeholder group has enough people at the meeting, or if you can find others who will work with you, then it is a very good idea to set up a rota of floor managers for each of the negotiation sessions. The *Earth Negotiations Bulletin* produces a very good summary of delegates' statements the following day; but if you are there to lobby, you need to know what is happening as it happens. Floor managers play a critical role. They can:

- note what each government is saying about a particular issue;
- help to identify the countries causing obstacles to action;
- help to identify who might be a broker for a solution;
- identify who is working/negotiating with whom;
- act as a focal point for lobbyists who are coming in and out of the meeting and help them to identify the next delegate to lobby; and
- provide an analysis to the group as a whole at any point during the process.

For a floor manager to be effective, he or she needs some key resources:

- an agreed framework for collecting information;
- if possible, a laptop to save time in writing up;
- a mobile telephone and the mobile phone numbers of the lobbyists working on a particular issue;
- a photo journal of key negotiators so that they can identify who is talking; and
- access to a digital camera; if someone is not in the photo listing and is taking an active role, then go up after a session and ask if you can take a photo.

Floor managing can be critical to the success of any lobbying team and offers newcomers the chance to understand the process more quickly than if just focusing on one issue.

Dinners

Some NGOs use dinners as a means of connecting with governments and sharing ideas. In 1998 a number of NGOs twice brought together a group of 10 to 12 governments to discuss what went wrong at the five-year review for the Earth Summit (Rio +5) and what could be done to make the ten-year review in Johannesburg in 2002 different. Out of this they drew up a 'non-paper': a paper that tries to capture the ideas of those who took part. Many governments used this as a basis for their own internal discussions and the International Chamber of Commerce reviewed it in 1999 to see what the impact of the ideas would be on industry.

Another example was a stakeholder dinner held in 2003 for governments to discuss a paper that the stakeholders had produced on the future of the Commission on Sustainable Development (CSD). The object of the dinner was to explore the ideas in the paper to see if they would find resonance with governments. The paper was produced six months before the meeting at which the CSD's future would be discussed; therefore, government ideas were not well developed. The paper produced was used to kick off governments' internal discussions, which then fed into revised versions of the paper. With this alternative paper being produced, it also acted as a counterbalance of ideas to those from the UN Secretariat.

There may be many objectives for organizing dinners. Just the recognition that an NGO is trying to help governments to think creatively in a particular area can pay great dividends when those NGOs are lobbying. Governments look for those who are continually interested in dialogue with them, not just arguing their own ideas. Many governments have neither the resources nor the time to do the work that they would like on a particular issue. Dinners are an opportunity to informally explore some of the gaps.

Government consultations

If you think that your organization has an issue that is critical to the negotiations, then you can call your own informal meeting and invite governments. This can be before or during the international meeting; invite key governments to discuss your idea. At the Habitat conference,

NGOs called a meeting in London to look at institutional follow-up. Each UN region selected a country to attend the two-day workshop, which dealt with a very controversial issue.[6] The outcome from the workshop was that G77 changed its position in line with that which NGOs were advocating.

How To Attend and Participate in UN Meetings

In order to participate in a UN commission, conference or summit, your organization primarily needs to be accredited to the UN Economic and Social Council (ECOSOC) or to the conference itself. The conventions and UN agencies have their own accreditation process.

If it is a conference or summit process and you are not accredited to ECOSOC, then there is an advantage of going through requesting accreditation to ECOSOC at the same time as getting accredited to a summit or conference.

The process of getting accredited to ECOSOC can take up to two years. The accreditation will have to go through the Committee on Non-Governmental Organizations. It meets only once a year in two parts, usually during May and June. It is best to include a number of countries that are less sympathetic to NGO representation.

If you are attending a UN conference or summit and are already accredited through ECOSOC, then you only need to fill in a pre-registration form, as all of those already accredited to ECOSOC will be automatically accredited to the summit.

If you just accredit to the conference or summit, then you will only be allowed to attend the preparatory meetings and actual meeting, and after this your accreditation will cease.

To start the process for accreditation to ECOSOC, you need to go to the web page www.un.org/esa/coordination/ngo/documents.htm to download the relevant form. The site also includes a model application form to help you understand how to apply. Organizations have been refused accreditation because they filled the form in badly. You can ask your government's mission to look at your application form in advance. It will usually pick up any obvious problems. In certain areas, NGO coalitions will have staff who will also do this for you.

There are three levels of accreditation to ECOSOC. These are general, special and roster (see Table 3.2).

Note of warning! 'Umbrella' or coalition NGOs should be careful about their member organizations. One gay rights coalition ran into opposition from the governmental NGO committee because it had

Table 3.2 *Differences in UN NGO status*

Privileges/obligations	General	Special	Roster
Relevance to the work of ECOSOC	all areas	some areas	limited
Are in consultative status with ECOSOC	yes	yes	yes
Designate UN representatives	yes	yes	yes
Invited to UN conferences	yes	yes	yes
Propose items for ECOSOC agenda	yes	no	no
Can speak at ECOSOC	yes	no	no
Attend UN meetings	yes	yes	yes
Circulate statements at ECOSOC meetings	2000 words	500 words	no
Circulate statements at ECOSOC subsidiary bodies' meetings	2000 words	500 words	no
Can speak at ECOSOC subsidiary bodies' meetings	yes	yes	no
Must submit quadrennial reports	yes	yes	no

Source: UN Division for Economic and Social Affairs, NGO Section, www.un.org/esa/coordination/ngo

(inadvertently, it claimed) allowed into membership a paedophile organization.

Representatives accredited by the umbrella group must be made aware that they will be deemed to be speaking for the umbrella and not just for their own organization. If, while making a verbal intervention, they start speaking in terms of their own group, the chair may well stop them. This can result in the large NGOs or coalitions being accused by small NGOs that they accredit of exercising a veto over what they want to say.

Likewise, the umbrella organization should insist on knowing just who is speaking – one NGO had to struggle hard to keep its consultative status after a member group fielded the leader of the rebel army. The official representatives of the government of the country concerned objected strongly. The borderline between an opposition political party and a partisan or minority rights group is hard to draw. National political parties cannot gain UN consultative status, but international political groupings can – for example, the UK Liberal Democrat party: no; Liberal International: yes.

Accreditation

You must be accredited by an ECOSOC-accredited NGO to attend a UN meeting.

The ECOSOC-accredited NGO must write to the UN, to inform them that you are going to attend, at least three weeks before you arrive. This should be done on their headed note paper and should be sent to the NGO section of the Department for Economic and Social Affairs' (DESA's) Division for ECOSOC Support and Coordination. For a UN conference or summit, a separate process may be set up or they may use the NGO section. For a convention or a UN agency, each will have its own processes and focal points. The UN Non-Governmental Liaison Service (NGLS) can help you with this if you are unsure.[7]

Depending upon the number of NGOs accredited for the meeting, it is possible that a special desk will be set up in the UN visitors' entrance for the first day. If this is not the case, then you may have to go to the relevant NGO section, where they will check your application and stamp your letter accordingly. They should have sent you a confirmation of your application to attend the meeting. If they have not, then it is crucial to take the letter that you sent to them. You can then collect your pass from the Pass Office at the north-west corner of 45th Street and 1st Avenue. You will need to take the following with you:

- your passport;
- a copy of the accreditation letter you sent; and
- a copy of any reply received.

If you are arriving early, it's worth accrediting then, to avoid the queues of the first day.

Chapter 4

How To Be Effective

Before You Arrive

- Discuss the agenda of the meeting within your NGO/stakeholder group and among others in your field. A well-organized back-up by other NGOs/stakeholders in your country can mean pressure being put on the government at home, as well as at the UN meeting. You may want to set up a rapid reaction group who can take action on an issue within your parliament or with national newspapers.
- Place opinion articles in the key monthly journals about the issues on which you are campaigning. Focus, in particular, on those journals that you know the minister or civil servants read.
- Meet with the major journalists who are likely to write for the daily and Sunday newspapers, as well as those for the radio and TV programmes. This can be done through a formal press conference.
- Research the members of the key country delegations whom you wish to lobby.
- Ensure government representatives have a copy of your views at least six weeks before a UN meeting.
- Ensure you have a copy of the latest text that is being discussed. This will be on the UN website (and should be posted at least six weeks before the meeting). Ensure that you have provided governments with your view on this text within a week of the text being posted.
- Do an analysis of proposals against previous agreements.
- It pays to read all of the background documents and relevant previous agreements. Some members of delegations will not have

done this; as a result, you can become a great source of knowledge.
- As the text develops, always have short text suggestions that build on previous UN agreements, which you can give to delegations.
- Whichever issue your NGO/stakeholder group wants to focus on, you should think about all of the possible outcomes, not just the ones you would like to see. You need to know the full range of these views, and how to counter views with which you do not agree.
- Contribute to the broader preparation of any issue caucus or stakeholder coalition, which is usually done by list server. They should also be working to similar timelines.
- Find out the name of the relevant officials in each government mission and send your views on the issues to the key governments.
- Send off your accreditation details at least three weeks before the meeting.
- Download photographs of the key delegates from the website so that you can identify them quickly.
- Bring with you, if you are able, a mobile office: computer, printer, telephone, etc.
- Plan to meet with key government officials to discuss your position in the week before the meeting. If you cannot get to New York/Geneva or where the meeting is being held, try telephoning for a chat.

At the UN Meeting

Often stakeholder representatives are the only delegates consistently attending, as government officials are moved on. Therefore, be aware of changing delegations as you may have to start from scratch again and again.

- Work with the NGOs/stakeholders present – it's impossible for an individual to cover everything. This is most effective if you have set it up before you arrive.
- The NGOs or stakeholder groups (for example, women's groups) usually organize a morning meeting before the negotiations start. This is where you can quickly find out what is happening and you can also share your information and discover who the key players are.
- In some negotiations, the NGOs/stakeholder groups will operate 'floor managers'. Their role is to take notes on the negotiations

and report back to the next NGO/stakeholder meeting. Get involved; it helps in understanding what is happening.

- As the official negotiating text develops, contribute to the production of suggested amendments to the text through NGO/stakeholder group position papers, as these tend to carry more weight than individual NGOs'/stakeholders' papers.
- Talk regularly to your government's delegation – tell them your priorities and suggest text amendments.
- Work with the NGOs/stakeholders on your government's delegation to ensure that they are putting forward agreed positions.
- Target other governments.
- As the negotiations progress, talk to those not in a bloc. It is easier to persuade one government to take on your ideas rather than a bloc. Target countries that tend to act individually – for example, Australia, Canada, Japan, New Zealand, Norway, Switzerland and the US.
- If your country works in a bloc, you will need to convince more than your own government to adopt your amendments – for example, the EU has 15 governments to convince.
- Don't overlook countries with economies in transition, as they are also possible targets. Some of the more progressive will be joining the EU in 2004. Of those left, it is worth creating a relationship with the Ukraine, Romania and Russia.
- Be aware of the considerable pressures on delegates and their interests. Remember this can be a two-way process – share information that might be of use to the delegate you are meeting. As well as getting your own point across, this makes for a stronger relationship.
- Make informal contacts with the delegations. Much effective lobbying work happens informally. Key places are:
  - coffee shops in the UN complexes – for example, the Vienna Café in New York and the Geneva Lounge in Geneva;
  - delegates lounge; this is meant to be only for delegates; but you may enter with a delegate wearing either a yellow badge (head of delegation); red badge (member of a delegation) or blue badge (member of an intergovernmental organization accredited to the UN General Assembly);
  - delegates dining room;
  - corridors;
  - back of meeting rooms;
  - main cafeteria;
  - government missions.

Successful lobbying is fun but can seem very daunting for a beginner. It is important to remember a few rules:

- When you meet a government official, give them your card and ask for theirs.
- The main discussion is often very procedural and can be a bit boring, so government delegates are often pleased to be asked to go for a coffee. Explain who you are and that you would like to share some ideas for section/issue X with them. Don't go in aggressively or forcefully.
- Find out who they are as a person, as well as their work – you may be surprised at what you find out and could make a friend as opposed to someone just to lobby. Try to pick a neutral issue to start the conversation – it could be sport or something about their country – for example, perhaps you've been there and something funny happened to you. One that the author used during the negotiations on the oceans chapter of Agenda 21 was that I had just been published in *Fish Fryers Review*, the monthly magazine of the fish and chip shops in the UK. This led to amusing discussions on the UK's contribution to gastronomy before moving on to serious issues on food stocks.
- Find out which issue the official has responsibility for in the delegation.
- Don't approach them in the meeting room if they are speaking or their country placard is raised, as they will have to speak.
- Governments are interested in finding out what NGO/stakeholder groups think and also what is happening in the corridors. You can help them with this.
- When giving some information about what you want, you need to be very specific. If you want text in a particular place, then provide material that shows the preferred text and where it should go. A general rule is to insert the text you want as bold text; or if you want something deleted, mark this as bold with the word 'delete' in front. Here is an example:

Governments and international bodies alone cannot achieve sustainable development. (Insert: **It needs active support and participation by stakeholders of all kinds and at all levels***.) At the Johannesburg Summit, we have welcomed a range of new partnership activities involving (Delete:* **governments***) stakeholders to promote sustainability in a variety of ways. We shall ensure that stakeholders of all kinds* *are further involved in the formulation of regional, national and local sustainable development strategies, and commit to support their role in implementation.*

- If you are dealing with text that appears in brackets, understand what they mean (see 'The World of Brackets' on p67).
- A rule of thumb: if you are spending more time with your own group than with government officials, review your work pattern. A good way to do this is to work out your daily timetable and proportion out time for NGO/stakeholder work at no more than 25 per cent. It will tend to creep up; but remember that you are there to lobby, not to spend time with your colleagues.
- If you have a team of people lobbying, agree who will talk to whom. Governments do not wish to be lobbied by lots of people over the same issue; but do let them know how many organizations support your view. It is useful if you are working on an issue to have people assigned to look after the EU presidency, G77 and countries that have single decisions.
- If you have a problem with certain governments, invite those you think can be convinced to a meeting to discuss your idea. This can be in the building for drinks or dinner. Those that are unable to attend can be dealt with individually. This also applies the other way round – governments that like your idea can be brought together to form a coalition.
- Try to be positive at all times.
- Governments operate every day by sending what is called a 'telegraph' back to their capital to explain what is happening and ask for instructions on areas that have come up. This is an excellent way of keeping your allies linked in and gives them the chance to be active in the media or to support your lobbying.
- Every day, try to extend the number of individuals from different countries to whom you talk.
- At some point, a list of people attending the meeting will be published by the UN – keep an eye open for this as it will help you to identify people whom you should see.
- If you're on a government delegation, especially for the first time, there can be a lot going on and important information can be easy to miss. Ask for a copy of the government brief. Also ask for the daily 'telegraph' that they are sending back to capitals.
- If there are other stakeholders on your government delegation, try to distribute tasks with them. Try to find stakeholders on other government delegations and work with them as well.

- If you are on delegation, you can play a key role in helping the government to understand what is happening within the stakeholder group whom you represent. You can also share information that you hear on the floor. It can sometimes be easier for opposing government delegations to talk to a stakeholder group representative as an intermediary in order to move ideas forward.
- Do not at any point sit in a government seat at a formal meeting unless you are on a government delegation and have been asked by your government to do so.
- Don't just think about the meeting at hand, but about the ones to follow – putting in place the building blocks that lead to sustainable results. This isn't just thinking about the words on paper, but also about the relationships and the networking (again, don't overlook business, secretariats, international organizations, etc).
- It is quite possible that the negotiations will not end on the date or time indicated. Therefore, if you can, plan to stay until the Sunday after the official meeting end in case they go through the Friday night.

FOLLOW-UP

When you get home, this may be at the end of a process or still in the middle of one:

- If it is at the end of a process – for example, a summit – then take two weeks off as you may feel very down and miss the adrenalin rush. Everyone feels a downer after intense negotiations; a summit process is probably the worst and many personal relationships suffer during this time. If you can recognize what is going to happen, the impact will be less.
- Organize a debriefing with individuals in your NGO/stakeholder group.
- Organize a meeting with the government to discuss follow-up or next stages.
- Do follow up emails with the government officials whom you met, just saying what you thought came out of the meeting and thanking them for supporting your ideas and for the work that they did.
- Write an article for relevant monthly publications so that you can share the outcomes with as many people as possible.

- Follow up with the UN Secretariat to see what they are planning; in an ongoing process you may find that there are informal meetings planned in New York or Geneva.
- If there does not yet exist a coalition to follow up internationally, then it is important to set one up. This, in particular, allows support for small NGOs and those that are not used to the UN process. An example of this was the CSD NGO Steering Committee (1994–2001). Although it no longer exists, its material is a useful example, and can be accessed online at http://csdngo.igc.org/sitemap.htm.[1]

THE NEGOTIATIONS: SOME TIPS

This section explains the formal side of what happens in a negotiation. Although people are representing organizations, each individual will have their own specialities; but the following should hold as generic. This section also provides some thoughts for those on the government negotiating team.

For governments, negotiations need to start early, particularly if they are in a bloc of countries. They should also be testing the water with delegates from countries with whom they are going to negotiate in order to see where the range of agreements is. Negotiations are not linear in their application; they are, by nature, a messy process and it is even difficult for governments to keep abreast of what is happening at times. If you are a government official, you need to be clear of your range of acceptable positions.

Formal sessions of a UN meeting (Committee of the Whole) are governed by rules of procedure and are conducted in all of the six UN languages.[2] These meetings are open for all to attend: governments and stakeholders. It is impossible to negotiate in a plenary of (in some cases) over 200 countries. In such cases, the agenda of issues will usually require the setting up of subsidiary bodies. These could take the form of the following:

- **Working groups** are a subsidiary body to the Committee of the Whole (COW). At any one time, usually no more than two will be meeting.
- **Informals** are a subsidiary body of the working groups and are set up when there is a set of critical issues that needs to be addressed.
- **Contact groups** are set up to resolve a particular issue of disagreement. The members of the group are drawn from the

governments who disagree, although they are open to others to attend. In negotiations there is usually a limit to the subsidiary bodies created. One reason for this is that small delegations cannot possibly have the staff support to enable them to cover multiple meetings (usually the largest delegation attending will be from the US). Another is that when it gets down to trading, this keeps the trading simple enough to deal with. Although there is usually an agreement that there will be no more than two working groups meeting at one time, these may spawn contact groups; but even these will be kept to a small number at any one time.

For something to be agreed, it needs to be agreed by the COW in a formal session. If there has been an agreement in a contact group, it will be passed up to possibly an informal, then to a working group and finally to COW. It is only the COW that can adopt an agreement, as it is only this committee that represents all of the countries involved. It should be noted that sessions below working groups might be conducted only in English. Informals and contact group meetings will certainly only be in English.

Rules of procedure

All UN meetings will have rules of procedure – these are, in the case of ECOSOC functioning commissions, set by ECOSOC and, ultimately, the UN General Assembly. For UN conferences and summits, the UN General Assembly sets the rules of procedures. The Conference of the Parties (COP) does this for a convention.

These rules cover everything from the role that stakeholders can play, to the election of the bureau and the role of the secretariat.

For delegates to speak, they need to put up their country placard. This is usually to put forward their position, although often this will be done through a bloc (for example, the EU or the G77). They may also want to make a point of order. Different meetings use different ways of doing this; but the most common procedure is to put the placard up and indicate a T with your arms. (One US delegate who will remain nameless, as he is Stakeholder Forum's co-chair, used two of the US placards and banged them together to get the chair's attention!)

For stakeholders, there will also be a placard. Usually in meetings in the area of sustainable development, these will be based on the Agenda 21 Major Groups; in others it may just be an NGO placard.

The object of the negotiations is to come to a consensus. This may not always be possible, in which case – depending upon the forum –

countries can ask for reservations to be published as footnotes to a particular issue that could not be agreed upon. If this is a conference, then it will be referred to ECOSOC and, ultimately, to the UN General Assembly. If issues go down this track, it is very unusual for them to have a better hearing in ECOSOC as these meetings will be populated by foreign ministries. In conventions, there can be majority voting, two-thirds voting or weighted voting. If you don't know what system is being used, ask the secretariat.

It is vital that countries have at least one good English-speaking delegate on their delegation. Many of the sessions will be in English only and they will need to understand the subtle differences between changing words in order to put forward their country's position effectively. It helps, particularly in the G77 coordination meetings, to have text that you want to propose written down and circulated. This also helps to balance against the more vocal members of the G77.

It is important to have with you all of the previous decisions taken in the area that you are negotiating. In addition, look back at your group's previous position and have copies of that with you. This gives you access to already agreed language and helps you to understand when other countries are trying to either move forward or to revise a previous decision. If you are in a group meeting of either the G77 or the EU and do not speak up, the assumption will be that you agree, even if you do not.

NGO/STAKEHOLDER PAPERS AND STATEMENTS

There are a number of formal ways in which an NGO/stakeholder group can participate in the summit negotiations. These include:

Individual stakeholder/stakeholder group position papers:

Your organization will arrive with a position on the issues that you are prioritizing for the meeting. These may be in the form of background papers or focused points that you want governments to look at. An interesting approach to this was taken for the Rio +5 meeting by NGOs, where they produced two documents. These were a top-ten set of issues and a larger compilation of NGO views with a common structure for each issue. This common structure was:

Box 4.1 NGOs' priority issues at the Rio + 5 UN General Assembly Special Session (UNGASS) (23–27 June 1997)

The NGO positions were as follows:[3]

1 CO_2 Climate

Agree to a legally binding commitment to reduce CO_2 emissions to 20 per cent below 1990 levels by the year 2000, and other appropriate reductions in greenhouse gases, at Kyoto, Japan, in December 1997, including special initiatives to protect and compensate small island developing states:

→ ✗ Result: not achieved

2002 update:

- Following Rio +5, the Third Conference of the Parties (COP-3) was held in Kyoto on 1–11 December 1997 and adopted the Kyoto Protocol, an agreement to commitments with a view to reducing overall emissions of six greenhouse gases by at least 5 per cent below 1990 levels between 2008 and 2012.
- At COP-6 (July 2001) agreement was reached on elements of an emissions trading system to allow flexibility in meeting the overall target. At COP-7, governments adopted the Marrakech Accords, finalizing the operational details of the Kyoto Protocol. Canada has become the 99th country to ratify the Kyoto Protocol on reducing greenhouse gas emissions. The move means that if, as promised, Russia now signs, the 1997 agreement will have achieved a critical mass and finally come into force.

2 Toxic Chemicals

Ensure that the legally binding persistent organic pollutants (POPs) global instrument is concluded and opened for ratification by 2000, at the latest, and that industrialized countries make a concerted effort in the next 12 months to assist developing nations for the Intergovernmental Negotiating Committee (INC) that will meet in early 1998:

→ ✔ Result: achieved

2002 update:

- Following Rio +5, there have been two rounds of negotiations towards an international treaty (a legally binding instrument) on POPs beginning in June to July 1998 and in January 1999.
- The INC and its subsidiary bodies completed work on the instrument, the Stockholm Convention on Persistent Organic Pollutants, in December 2000. The convention was adopted and opened for signature in May 2001. The convention will enter into force 90 days after the submission of the 50th instrument of ratification by a government. There are currently 151 signatories and 26 ratifications.

3 Forests

Commit to the continuation and enhancement of the intergovernmental policy dialogue on forests under the CSD, while also promoting (in a transparent and participatory manner) an action-oriented programme to solve critical forest-related problems involving all types of forests, including a halt to further destruction of primary and old-growth forests around the world, and the establishment of networks of ecologically representative and socially appropriate forest protected areas (covering at least 10 per cent of the world's forests) by 2000:

→ ✔ Result: achieved

2002 update:

- Rio +5 review recommended continuation of the intergovernmental policy dialogue on forests through the establishment of an ad-hoc open-ended Intergovernmental Forum on Forests.
- More than 270 proposals for action towards sustainable forest management were put forward. Although these proposals for action are not legally binding, participants of these processes are under a political obligation to implement the agreed proposals for action, and each country is expected to conduct a systematic national assessment of the proposals and to plan for their implementation. In 2000, the UN Forum on Forests (UNFF) was established by ECOSOC as part of a new international arrangement on forests to carry on the work building on the Intergovernmental Panel on Forests (IPF) and the Intergovernmental Forum on Forests (IFF) processes. The forum held its first session in June 2001. It adopted three

resolutions concerning its multi-year programme of work during 2001 to 2005: the development of a plan of action and its work with the Collaborative Partnership on Forests, and one decision concerning the accreditation of intergovernmental organizations. An outcome of the WSSD in 2002 was to accelerate the implementation of the IPF/IFF proposals for action by countries and by the Collaborative Partnership on Forests, and to intensify efforts on reporting to the UNFF to contribute to an assessment of progress in 2005. Three forest-related partnerships were launched at the summit.

4 Freshwater

Initiate negotiations on a global agreement or arrangement on freshwater by 1998 with terms of reference that include a commitment to a catchments (watershed/airshed) approach as the basis for action on freshwater in national sustainable development strategies and any international plan or strategies:

➜ ✗ Result: not achieved

2002 update:

- The five-year review found conflict on water rights, and regional and political disputes too hot an issue to address. Originally, the Bonn Freshwater Conference in 2001 was to address this issue; but it also found it too difficult and looked at other areas. Water moved up the political agenda from Rio +5 and, as well as the Bonn conference, there was a report from the World Water Commission and the World Water Forum in The Hague, which contributed informally to the preparations of Rio +10.
- At the WSSD it was stated that, by the year 2015, the proportion of people who are unable to reach or to afford safe drinking water should be halved, as outlined in the Millennium Declaration. A programme of actions, with financial and technical assistance, will be launched to achieve this goal. Furthermore, integrated water resources management and water efficiency plans are to be developed by 2005, with support to developing countries. It was also agreed that there should be a similar target for sanitation.

5 Military Weapons

Adopt a global legally binding ban on anti-personnel land mines by 1999, applicable both within and between countries, and a legally binding ban on the production and use of nuclear weapons by 2002:

→ ✗ Result: not achieved

2002 update:

- A global legally binding ban on anti-personnel land mines has not been agreed; however, more recently progress has been made. The First Meeting of the States Parties (FMSP) to the Convention on the Prohibition of the Use, Stockpiling, Production and Transfer of Anti-Personnel Mines and on their Destruction was held in Mozambique. The convention, already signed by 135 countries, entered into force on 1 March 1999.
- There are now 126 states that are party to the Ottawa Mine Ban Convention. At the Fourth Meeting of the States Parties in Japan 2002, it was noted that it was essential to promote the universal support of the convention. 2003 is the deadline for the first group of states parties to destroy all stockpiled anti-personnel mines. The first review conference will be held in 2004.

Cross-sectoral issues included the following.

6 Finance

Establish an Intergovernmental Panel on Finance at the UN Special Session with terms of reference that include the need to create innovative mechanisms for NGOs and civil society access to capital, credit and capacity-building for community-based sustainable and environmentally sound economic development projects. Industrialized countries should provide substantial additional financial resources in support of sustainable development to the developing countries by 2000, including a 50 per cent increase in the current replenishment of the Global Environmental Facility (GEF). They should undertake targeted debt reductions in 20 of the most heavily indebted least developed countries by the end of 1998 in exchange for significant initiatives to further sustainable development. Industrialized countries should meet the 0.7 per cent of gross national product (GNP) target for aid by 2002 and achieve one half of that target (0.35 per cent) by the end of 1998.

Furthermore, all of the countries should take steps to ensure, by no later then 1998, stricter scrutiny, including new laws or other measures, to prevent the abuse of all funds and corrupt practices – in the public and private sector – at national and international levels:

➜ Result ➜ Referred to ECOSOC

- Currently recognized in ad-hoc, open-ended Working Group on Financing for Development. The high-level International Inter-governmental Forum on Financing for Development will take place in 2001 and will have preparatory meetings that will discuss mobilization of resources for development. The debt-relief movement, particularly the faith-based Jubilee 2000 Coalition, has greatly helped to raise public awareness and intensify debate reduction among the Group of 7 (G7) industrialized countries and the Russian Federation (G8).

➜ ✔ Result: GEF replenished

➜ ✔ Result: Canada and the UK are increasing aid, and the Nordic governments and the government of The Netherlands are still providing very high levels of aid

2002 update:

- As of November 2001, 24 countries are benefiting from heavily indebted poor countries (HIPC) relief, with several others in preparation.
- The outcome document of the International Conference on Financing for Development in March 2002 was the Monterrey Consensus, which encourages greater flows of foreign investment to developing countries in support of sustainable development. An extra US$12 billion was announced, with a US$5 billion increase in aid from the US from 2004, and an additional US$7 billion from the EU.
- The third replenishment of the GEF was concluded at the WSSD. The GEF is intended to cover projects of benefit to the global environment only; therefore, its use must be resisted to finance projects of solely domestic benefit.

7 Trade

Adopt a clear, internationally agreed, understanding by 1998 that environment conventions and other Multilateral Environmental

Agreements (MEAs) shall not be bound by World Trade Organization (WTO)-imposed requirements or restrictions (given that such WTO measures have, with few expectations, undermined those important agreements). In addition, convene a trade and environment ministers' summit before the next ministerial meeting of the WTO, which includes a discussion on fair trade versus free trade; and take steps to adopt measures, applicable to the next WTO ministerial meeting, that ensure transparency and effective opportunities for NGOs and other Major Groups to observe and contribute to those deliberations:

→ ✗ Result: not achieved

2002 update:

- The November 2001 Declaration of the Fourth Ministerial Conference in Doha, Qatar, provides the mandate for negotiations on a range of subjects, as well as other work, including issues concerning the implementation of the present agreements. This Doha Development Agenda includes negotiations aimed at reducing or eliminating tariffs and non-tariff barriers, especially on products of export interest to developing countries. Further liberalization in agriculture, through improvements in market access, reductions and eventual phasing-out of export subsidies, as well as substantial reduction in trade-distorting domestic support measures, are key priorities.
- The Programme of Action for the Least Developed Countries for the decade 2001 to 2010, adopted at the Third United Nations Conference for Least Developed Countries (Brussels, May 2001), seeks to arrest and reverse the continued socio-economic marginalization of least developed countries (LDCs), improve their share in international trade, foreign direct investment and other financial flows, and create an enabling environment for them to be able to benefit from globalization, as well as minimize its adverse consequences.

8 Corporate Accountability

To establish a sub-commission of the CSD at the UN Special Session to enact internationally agreed, government-based mechanisms by no later then 1999 that are designed to ensure significantly greater accountability of business and industry, especially transnational corporations:

→ ✗ Result: not achieved

2002 update:

- In 1998, the CSD set up an unsuccessful multi-stakeholder process to review voluntary initiatives.
- Industry, often through industry associations, has developed codes of conduct, charters and codes of good practice concerning social and environmental performance. The corporate responsibility movement is widening in developed countries, where firms are finding that better working conditions and more consultative forms of management result in improved economic and environmental performance.
- The WSSD called to actively promote corporate responsibility and accountability, based on the Rio Principles, including the full development and effective implementation of inter-governmental agreements and measures, international initiatives and public–private partnerships, and appropriate national regulations. It also encouraged continuous improvement in corporate practices in all countries.

9 Indigenous Peoples

Establish at the UN Special Session a Permanent Forum for Indigenous Peoples, within the UN system (under the CSD), to coordinate all international initiatives on indigenous peoples:

→ ✗ Result: not achieved

2002 update:

- In February 1999, an ad-hoc working group met in Geneva to discuss the proposal. The 17th session of the Working Group on Indigenous Populations, the largest international gathering of indigenous peoples in the world, also held its annual meeting in Geneva in July 1999 and proposed numerous initiatives to the United Nations.
- A second ad-hoc working group met in February 2000 to finalize a proposal for the Commission on Human Rights. At its 56th session, the Commission on Human Rights decided to recommend to ECOSOC that it set up a permanent forum on indigenous issues. On 28 July 2000, ECOSOC adopted a resolution establishing the Permanent Forum on Indigenous Issues. The purpose of the permanent forum is to serve as an advisory body to ECOSOC, with a mandate to discuss

indigenous issues relating to economic and social development, culture, the environment, education, health and human rights.

10 NGO Access

Ensure that the arrangements for the UN General Assembly Special Session (UNGASS) are, at minimum, based on the newly revised Arrangements for Consultation with Non-Governmental Organizations – Part VII of Resolution 1996/31 – and that these arrangements apply to strengthening NGO access to, and participation in, the UN General Assembly subsidiary bodies, including adequate representation by NGOs and other Major Groups from the South:

→ ✔ Result: achieved

2002 update:

- At Rio +5, Ambassador Razali (president of the UN General Assembly for the Special Session) was successful in securing extensive access for NGOs to UNGASS. Ten NGO presentations were made in the formal CSD sessions, and rights of access were on a par with those of formal CSD sessions. These arrangements were secured on the understanding (from the US and others) that they set no precedent for ongoing UN General Assembly (GA) work, so the second half of the objective has not been met.
- There was advanced involvement of stakeholders, including discussions and dialogues before and at the WSSD. The nine Major Groups identified in Agenda 21 spent four and a half days discussing three themes among themselves and with governments: review/assessment of progress (PrepCom 2); future priorities and partnership approaches (PrepCom 4); and multi-stakeholder implementation partnerships and commitments (during the WSSD).

Source: adapted from Dodds, McCoy and Tanner (1997)

- we call for...;
- implementation; and
- rationale.

This helped governments to understand what was wanted, who was going to do it and why it was important. Many NGOs/stakeholder groups have a tendency to put out a lot of information; but government delegates have limited ability to take lots of information in. This is particularly true as negotiations move towards the end game. It is important to have in-depth information available; but do not swamp them with it.

An example of the approach would be the second document that NGOs gave out in 1997, as presented in Box 4.1. This was their top-ten issues paper.

What can be seen from Box 4.1 is that over five years, NGOs continued their lobbying in other meetings to the point where many of the original priorities were largely achieved. When campaigning for a particular issue, it is vital to ensure that you have many places in which to raise the issue. This creates a momentum that is hard for governments to resist.

Agreed NGO/Major Group position papers

The UN provides tables outside the meeting room for organizations to put their papers on. Although this is a good place to distribute your material, it is as important to meet with government officials and give the material to them personally while discussing your ideas.

In the lead-up to the meeting, NGOs/stakeholder groups will try to agree a joint position paper. Because these papers represent a wider range of NGOs/stakeholder groups and their constituencies, they tend to carry greater weight with governments. If this is a summit process, then these papers may show a set of agreed text amendments. As we have shown on page 42, the usual format is to reproduce the government text with NGO/stakeholder group amendments in bold. This helps the delegates to understand what you want added and where.

Oral statements

ECOSOC-accredited NGOs/Major Groups may ask to make a brief oral statement to the meeting. These are at the discretion of the chair and with consent of the governments. The Commission on Sustainable Development process has allowed a great degree of contributions from stakeholders (Major Groups is the term that they use) during the negotiations. Usually, coordinated joint statements by a group of NGOs or stakeholder groups will be more likely to be allowed than statements by individual NGOs. Although, according to the rules, it should only be accredited organizations, governments understand the benefit of a coordinated statement and it is usually given more prominence than those of individual organizations. The statements are most effective if they are brief (less than five minutes) and substantive in nature. Some processes will allow comments on the text; others will not and will expect a set of broader comments. Make sure that you know which is allowed otherwise the chair may terminate your presentation.

Thirty copies of your statement must be given to the secretariat for the interpreters. If you want your statement given out to the governments, you cannot give it out yourself. You need to give 300 copies to the secretariat staff. You can also put extra copies on a table in the room with other statements.

Too often, stakeholders take a long time agreeing what they will say in a statement, thinking that this is going to make a difference. It will not. I can only think of a couple of occasions where the statement of a stakeholder in a session has caused a reaction that had not already been achieved by lobbying in the corridors.

Remember that governments often do not talk to each other. Within the EU, it is the presidency that represents the views of the Union, and it tends to be the civil servants who are expected to do the networking. The reality is they have their hands full with coordinating the 15 countries in the EU. Often, the EU is not doing the corridor work of talking with individual governments to help build the trust to move forward the issues. Direct contact between some of the governments sometimes breaks down.

Some examples of this include the following:

- One of the very interesting developments in the Habitat conference process was the informals that were held in Nairobi and Paris. The meeting treated stakeholders in a similar manner to governments, allowing them to enter text. The text became alive if a government agreed with it. Some amendments were put forward as joint government NGO/stakeholder amendments. Another development was the use of stakeholders to chair informal meetings. One NGO-chaired informal on the issue of transport disappeared to the pub and returned after a couple of pints with an agreement!
- For a CSD meeting, we had brought over a representative of an NGO working on human settlement issues. At the end of the first week I was playing pool at a party and he came over to chat. I asked: 'How is it going?' 'Bad!' was the reply, which surprised me as I thought it was going very well. I asked him: 'What have you been doing?' He said that he had taken part in an NGO meeting

over the previous weekend and agreed on a position. I then asked what had he done. He said that the group had put the NGO paper at the back of the negotiating room, and then he sat listening to the negotiations and couldn't understand why more of the NGO ideas hadn't been taken up. 'Oh!' I said. 'Did you notice the people talking at the back of the room?' He said he did. I said: 'They were lobbying! Did you notice the people in the coffee bar?' He said he did. I responded: 'They were lobbying!' Flippantly, I added: 'Did you notice the people going to the toilet?' and again he agreed that he had. I said: 'They were lobbying!' I asked if he knew Tony Simpson (a highly effective Australian NGO representative); he said that he did. I responded: 'Well, follow him about and observe whatever he does!'

I thought this was good advice until late Monday morning. Tony, a large guy who looks like an Australian rugby player, came over to me as I was walking between the conference rooms. He put his arm around my shoulders and said: 'We have to talk!' He asked if I had told this UK NGO representative to follow him around. I had, of course, but I thought my advice was more to observe than to follow. He said, 'I cannot even go to the toilet without him following me!'

STRUCTURE OF A DOCUMENT

The structure of a document can be critical on a number of fronts. A well-structured document:

* enables gaps to be clearly identified;
* identifies problem areas to be focused upon; and
* allows for principles and mainstreaming to be integrated.

An example of this is the approach taken for the Johannesburg WSSD in 2002, when there was considerable disagreement between those managing the process and almost everyone else regarding the document structure. A number of organizations and the South African government put forward suggestions on how to structure the document. Stakeholder Forum's suggestions are an example (see Box 4.2).[4]

Unfortunately, this approach and those suggested by others did not happen and the WSSD agreement therefore suffers from a lack of structure. Many possible outcomes may have been lost because of this.

Box 4.2 A suggested structure for the Johannesburg Plan of Implementation

Each section of the agreement should set poverty eradication as an overarching theme. Furthermore, the sections should mainstream the following aims:

- the Rio Principles;
- sustainable production and consumption;
- the enhancement of globalization;
- the Millennium Development Goals;
- human rights;
- gender equity; and
- good governance.

Each section will be organized under the following structure:

- Introduction to the overarching topic: outline general issues/problems.
- Programme areas: identify priority issues – for example, renewable energy.
- Basis for action: chapters in Agenda 21, CSD decisions, Millennium Development Goals, setting of additional targets.
- Objectives: for each priority issue, outline aims and purpose for action – for example, to improve access to renewable energy or to improve trade policy for energy provision.
- Activities at all levels: international to local action, touching on priorities for existing institutions, roles of stakeholders and outlining new institutional areas.
- Means of implementation: including capacity-building, technology-sharing, education and training (targeting sustainable development).
- Financial resources: public (domestic and foreign, aid and investment) and private (business, foundations, NGOs and others).
- Timetable and targets: 5, 10 or 15 years.
- Information for decision-making: monitoring and assessing progress; indicators; data management and provision.

Lessons

The lesson from lobbying on this issue was that the discussions on structure happened far too late to enable the required outcome to occur. Although there were corridor discussions at the WSSD second

Preparatory Meeting, governments did not set time aside to have a discussion on structure. By the third Preparatory Meeting, it was virtually impossible to make any changes (even though Stakeholder Forum cut up the text and repackaged it to show what it would look like). In fact, the whole timetable for WSSD was too short – it did not allow for dealing with throwing out the text and starting again. For a conference and summit process with Regional PrepComs, the minimum time span should be two years.

In addition, there might be an argument for the UN General Assembly to agree to a standard draft structure for a UN conference programme of action, as opposed to letting each bureau for a conference start from scratch. Finally, a little bit of knowledge management would go a long way.

So You Want To Be an Activist?

Although this book is principally about lobbying, I can't resist including a small section on direct action for those NGOs or other stakeholders coming to add weight to their positions at the meetings. Although I would use less inflammatory language, I always think that any person undertaking direct action could do no better than to start by reading Saul Alinsky's book *Rules for Radicals* (Alinsky, 1971), which has a great section called 'Alinsky's Rules for Effective Tactics' (see Box 4.3).

As someone who started in the anti-apartheid movement during the 1970s, I am reminded of a story that Peter Hain[5] told in his excellent book *Don't Play with Apartheid: The Background to the Stop the Seventies Tour Campaign* (Hain, 1971) The story relates to Alinsky's first rule: 'Power is not only what you have, but what the enemy thinks you have.'

The story goes something like this. A London university biological student was planning to wreck the 1970 South African Cricket Tour of the UK with an army of locusts. He announced that he already had 50,000 of the insects at his house and would breed another 500,000 by the time the tourists arrived for the match. The student, David Wilton Godberford, was quoted in the London *Times* on 11 May as saying:

> *Anything up to 100,000 locusts will be let loose at a particular ground and I think the plan is foolproof. They will ravage every blade of grass and green foliage... So that their insatiable appetites will not be impaired, they will not be fed for 24 hours before the moment of truth... It takes 70,000 hoppers 12*

> ## Box 4.3 Alinsky's rules for effective tactics
>
> - Power is not only what you have, but also what the enemy thinks you have.
> - Never go outside the experience of your people. It may result in confusion, fear and retreat.
> - Wherever possible go outside the experience of the enemy. Here, you want to cause confusion, fear and retreat.
> - Make the enemy live up to his/her own book of rules.
> - Ridicule is man's most potent weapon.
> - A good tactic is one that your people enjoy.
> - A tactic that drags on too long becomes a drag.
> - Keep the pressure on, with different tactics and actions, and utilize all events of the period for your purpose.
> - The threat is usually more terrifying than the thing itself.
> - The major premise for tactics is the development of operations that will maintain a constant pressure upon the opposition.
> - If you push a negative hard and deep enough, it will break through into its counter side.
> - The price of a successful attack is a constructive alternative.
> - Pick the target, freeze it, personalize it and polarize it.

minutes to consume 50 kilograms of grass. The crack of a solid army of locusts feeding on the grass will sound like flames. The South Africans are going to dread this trip.

There were no questions in the press about how you might breed 500,000 locusts in student accommodation. No questions about how they would be able to get them into the ground. The reason for this was that all of the previous actions threatened by those in this campaign had been taken – so this was treated as a real possibility!

Direct action inside a UN meeting is *not* a good idea. This can negatively impact upon what you want to achieve. It can cause countries that are in support of your position, and those wavering, to pull back. You can have your NGO lose consultative status at the UN – which would impact upon your work forever. There are some direct action activities that are considered more 'soft'. During a number of events, stakeholders have conducted a mass walk inside, or all stakeholders stood up together during the negotiations to indicate non-support for an issue. The question, if you are doing direct action, is: who is your target? If it is a particular country or group of countries, then focus on them. Generally, this will involve gaining media attention to enable the public to understand an issue and to put pressure back in capitals.

If it is the media you are targeting, read the section on 'Media Campaigning' at the end of this chapter and remember that the more fun the direct action is, the more likely the media is to pick it up.

When engaging in direct action, always treat UN staff, government officials and, definitely, UN Security with great respect. Given the highly polarized political situation in the world today, it is important to recognize the difficult job they have to perform.

UN Security deals with stakeholders all of the time and has, on a number of occasions at UN conferences, protected those from actions by local police.

If you are planning direct action outside a meeting, a few things to think about are:

- Check the law in the country in which you are conducting the action.
- Have a local lawyer ready for those who might need help.
- Explain to those who are doing any action what might happen to them.
- Take next of kin details of all of those taking action.
- Have a photographer with you who does not take part in an action who can film or take pictures of what happens.
- Do *not* respond if you are hit.

Agreements, Charters, Conventions, Declarations, Protocols and Treaties[6]

Agreements

The term 'agreement' can have a generic and a specific meaning. It also has acquired a special meaning in the law of regional economic integration.

Agreement as a generic term

The 1969 Vienna Convention on the Law of Treaties employs the term 'international agreement' in its broadest sense. On the one hand, it defines treaties as international agreements with certain characteristics. On the other hand, it employs the term international agreements for instruments that do not meet its definition of 'treaty'. Its Article 3 also refers to 'international agreements not in written form'. Although such oral agreements may be rare, they can have the same binding force as treaties depending upon the intention of the parties. An example of an oral agreement might be a promise made by the minister of foreign affairs of one state to his counterpart of another state. Consequently, the term international agreement in its generic sense embraces the widest range of international instruments.

Agreement as a particular term

'Agreements' are usually less formal and deal with a narrower range of subject matter than 'treaties'. There is a general tendency to apply the term agreement to bilateral or restricted multilateral treaties. It is especially employed for instruments of a technical or administrative character that are signed by the representatives of government departments, but are not subject to ratification. Typical agreements deal with matters of economic, cultural, scientific and technical cooperation. Agreements also frequently deal with financial matters, such as avoidance of double taxation, investment guarantees or financial assistance. The UN and other international organizations regularly conclude agreements with the host country to an international conference or to a session of a representative organ of the organization. Particularly in international economic law, the term agreement is also used as a title for broad multilateral agreements (for example, the commodity agreements). The use of the term agreement slowly developed during the first decades of the 20th century. Today, by far the majority of international instruments are designated as agreements.

Agreements in regional integration schemes

Regional integration schemes are based on general framework treaties with constitutional character. International instruments that amend this framework at a later stage (for example, accessions and revisions) are also designated as 'treaties'. Instruments that are concluded within the framework of the constitutional treaty or by the organs of the regional organization are usually referred to as agreements in order to distinguish them from the constitutional treaty. For example, whereas the Treaty of Rome of 1957 serves as a quasi-constitution of the European Community (EC), treaties concluded by the EC with other nations are usually designated as agreements. Furthermore, the Treaty of Montevideo of 1980 established the Latin American Integration Association (LAIA); but the subregional instruments entered into under its framework are called agreements.

Charters

The term 'charter' is particularly used for formal and solemn instruments, such as the constitutional treaty of an international organization. The term itself has an emotive content that goes back to the Magna Carta of 1215. Well-known recent examples are the Charter of the United Nations of 1945 and the Charter of the Organization of American States of 1952.

Conventions

The term 'convention' again can have both a generic and a specific meaning.

Convention as a generic term

Article 38(1)(a) of the Statute of the International Court of Justice refers to 'international conventions, whether general or particular' as a source of law, apart from international customary rules and general principles of international law, and – as a secondary source – judicial decisions and the teachings of the most highly qualified publicists. This generic use of the term convention embraces all international agreements in the same way as the generic term 'treaty' does. Black-letter law is also regularly referred to as 'conventional law' in order to distinguish it from the other sources of international law, such as customary law or the general principles of international law. Thus, the generic term convention is synonymous with the generic term treaty.

Convention as a specific term

Whereas during the 20th century the term 'convention' was regularly employed for bilateral agreements, it now is generally used for formal multilateral treaties with a broad number of parties. Conventions are normally open for participation by the international community as a whole, or by a large number of states. Usually, the instruments negotiated under the auspices of an international organization are entitled conventions (for example, the Convention on Biological Diversity of 1992; the United Nations Convention on the Law of the Sea of 1982; and the Vienna Convention on the Law of Treaties of 1969). The same holds true for instruments adopted by an organ of an international organization (for example, the 1951 International Labour Organization Convention concerning Equal Remuneration for Men and Women Workers for Work of Equal Value, adopted by the International

Labour Conference or the 1989 Convention on the Rights of the Child, adopted by the UN General Assembly).

Declarations

The term 'declaration' is used for various international instruments. However, declarations are not always legally binding. The term is often deliberately chosen to indicate that the parties do not intend to create binding obligations, but merely want to declare certain aspirations. An example is the 1992 Rio Declaration. Declarations can, however, also be treaties in the generic sense, intended to be binding at international law. It is therefore necessary to establish in each individual case whether the parties intended to create binding obligations. Ascertaining the intention of the parties can often be a difficult task. Some instruments entitled declarations were not originally intended to have binding force; but their provisions may have reflected customary international law or may have gained binding character as customary law at a later stage. Such was the case with the 1948 Universal Declaration of Human Rights.

Protocols

The term 'protocol' is used for agreements less formal than those entitled 'treaty' or 'convention'. The term could be used to cover the following kinds of instruments:

- A *protocol of signature* is an instrument subsidiary to a treaty and is drawn up by the same parties. This kind of protocol deals with ancillary matters, such as the interpretation of particular clauses of the treaty, those formal clauses not inserted in the treaty, or the regulation of technical matters. Ratification of the treaty will normally *ipso facto* involve ratification of such a protocol.
- An *optional protocol to a treaty* is an instrument that establishes additional rights and obligations to a treaty. It is usually adopted on the same day, but is of independent character and subject to independent ratification. Such protocols enable certain parties of the treaty to establish among themselves a framework of obligations that reach further than the general treaty, and to which not all parties of the general treaty consent, creating a 'two-tier system'. The optional protocols to the International Covenant on Civil and Political Rights of 1966 are well-known examples.

- A *protocol based on a framework treaty* is an instrument with specific substantive obligations that implements the general objectives of a previous framework or umbrella convention. Such protocols ensure a more simplified and accelerated treaty-making process and have been used particularly in the field of international environmental law. An example is the 1987 Montreal Protocol on Substances that Deplete the Ozone Layer, adopted on the basis of Articles 2 and 8 of the 1985 Vienna Convention for the Protection of the Ozone Layer.
- A *protocol to amend* is an instrument that contains provisions that amend one or various former treaties, such as the protocol of 1946 amending the Agreements, Conventions and Protocols on Narcotic Drugs.
- A *protocol as a supplementary treaty* is an instrument that contains supplementary provisions to a previous treaty – for example, the 1967 protocol relating to the status of refugees to the 1951 Convention Relating to the Status of Refugees.
- A *process verbal* is an instrument that contains a record of certain understandings arrived at by the contracting parties.

Treaties

The term 'treaty' can be used as a common generic term or as a particular term that indicates an instrument with certain characteristics.

Treaty as a generic term

The term 'treaty' has regularly been used as a generic term embracing all instruments that are binding in international law and concluded between international entities, regardless of their formal designation. Both the 1969 and 1986 Vienna Conventions confirm this generic use of the term treaty. The 1969 Vienna Convention defines a treaty as 'an international agreement concluded between states in written form and governed by international law, whether embodied in a single instrument or in two or more related instruments and whatever its particular designation'. The 1986 Vienna Convention extends the definition of treaties to include international agreements involving international organizations as parties. In order to speak of a treaty in the generic sense, an instrument has to meet various criteria. First of all, it has to be a binding instrument, which means that the contracting parties intended to create legal rights and duties. Second, the instrument must be concluded by states or international organizations with treaty-making power. Third, it has to be governed by international law. Last, the engagement has to be in writing. Even before the 1969 Vienna Convention on the Law of Treaties, the word treaty in its generic sense had been generally reserved for engagements concluded in written form.

Treaty as a specific term

There are no consistent rules when state practice employs the term 'treaty' as a title for an international instrument. Usually, the term treaty is reserved for matters of some gravity that require more solemn agreements. Their signatures are usually sealed and they normally require ratification. Typical examples of international instruments designated as treaties are peace treaties, border treaties, delimitation treaties, extradition treaties, and treaties of friendship, commerce and cooperation. The use of the term treaty for international instruments has considerably declined in recent decades in favour of other terms.

THE WORLD OF BRACKETS

As the negotiations progress, the text becomes cluttered with brackets. These represent what has not yet been agreed. If you are involved with the negotiations it is very important to understand that there are many different types of brackets. They are not, however, presented differently in order to help anyone to understand what is happening! The different types include what might be descibed as follows:

- **Alternative brackets** comprise alternative text for the same issue and may revolve around a substantive disagreement, but tend to be similar wording for the same issue.
- **Contentious brackets** are there because of fundamental disagreement over a particular section.
- **Suspicious brackets** are used when one group thinks the other is up to something with a section or a phrase and therefore the brackets are put in until it becomes clearer.
- **Tactical or trading brackets** may be put in by one country to enable them to trade with another bracket in another section or in another area. It is important to understand what might be traded in order to unlock these brackets.
- **Uncertain brackets** are put where no one was quite sure what the proposed text meant or why the brackets were placed there in the first place.

- **Waiting brackets** are inserted when governments are waiting for instructions from the capital on what to do.
- **Weary brackets** are usually included when negotiations go on into the early morning and when people get too tired to negotiate effectively.[7]

Understanding the use of brackets is critical during a negotiation. Many stakeholder groups have not appreciated this in their preparations for a meeting or as the negotiating text goes through different revisions. Some guidance here might include:

1   Who put the bracket in?
2   When you know who put it forward, ask why.
3   The 'why' may not be clear to other delegations and you can play an important role in highlighting the 'why' in your lobbying.
4   Depending upon the answer to 'why', there may be different actions. These might include:
    - If it was because they are waiting for instructions from the capital, then phone your colleagues in the capital and get them to raise the issue with relevant civil servants or ministers. This only works if you are completely on top of the negotiations and can act immediately.
    - If it involves trading brackets with somewhere else in the text, then you need to be able to work with the stakeholders who are trying to lobby on that section.
    - If it is because of exhaustion brackets, then make some text suggestions. This can be a very opportunistic time as officials are tired and looking for a way through the darkness – or even to go home for the night!
    - If there are suspicious brackets, then it is important to work out why and try to help build trust.

Terms in Negotiations

When examining a UN resolution, you may be bewildered by the use of certain terms, and you are right to be so. Although confusing, they all have a particular meaning and it is vital that you appreciate what each is and what it means in relation to the use of other words. To help understand the terms, we have tried to explain what you might be reading (see Table 4.1).

How and why we communicate is key to the success of the interactions between people. In the case of negotiations, this is even

Table 4.1 Terms in negotiations

Term	Definition	Just the term – no action identified	Does it say who should do it?	Does it have timelines?	Does it have a monitoring mechanism?
Affirms	We are quite serious about this	✓	✓	✓	✓
Calls for	We are asking governments what they might consider doing	✓	✓	✓	✓
Calls upon	This is for someone else to do something	✓	✓	✓	✓
Concurs	We don't have to decide anything because some other body already did	✓	✓	✓	✓
Considers	We are not at all serious about this	✓	✓	✓	✓
Consults	We don't want to do anything about this at the moment	✓	✓	✓	✓
Cooperates	The more people we involve, the less will happen	✓	✓	✓	✓
Coordinates	It is a mess out there and unless we get people together nothing is going to happen	✓	✓	✓	✓
Decides	This is action! Someone – usually not governments – should do something	✓	✓	✓	✓
Develops	We suggest that someone does something some time in the future	✓	✓	✓	✓
Endorses	We think someone should do something we said they should have done before	✓	✓	✓	✓
Encourages	We hope someone is going to do something some time	✓	✓	✓	✓

Term	Definition	Just the term – no action identified	Does it say who should do it?	Does it have timelines?	Does it have a monitoring mechanism?
Enhances	We hope that these suggestions might make a difference in someone doing something	✓	✓	✓	✓
Establishes	Look, we can create something that might do something that we can't do at the moment	✓	✓	✓	✓
Expresses concern	We are really annoyed that something we asked for hasn't been done	✓	✓	✓	✓
Facilitates	We really need someone to help us	✓	✓	✓	✓
Implements	It's time to try to do what we said we would do	✓	✓	✓	✓
Maintains	We should at least do what we have been doing	✓	✓	✓	✓
Notes	This means it doesn't matter too much	✓	✓	✓	✓
Observes	Let's just watch	✓	✓	✓	✓
Promotes	We're pleased that someone else will do it	✓	✓	✓	✓
Provisional	We don't know if this is the right direction or not	✓	✓	✓	✓
Reaffirms	We still haven't done what we said we would do	✓	✓	✓	✓
Recalls	We said we would do something and we just remembered we haven't done it	✓	✓	✓	✓
Recognizes	We know there is a problem that we haven't yet addressed and probably don't have the money or political will to do so	✓	✓	✓	✓
Regulates	We are really serious this time	✓	✓	✓	✓

Requests	We are asking someone whom we have no right be asking to do something that they probably will not do	✓	✓	✓	✓
Restructures	It's a mess out there and if we don't hit some heads together nothing will happen	✓	✓	✓	✓
Revitalizes	It's not working – needs new energy and money	✓	✓	✓	✓
Revises	We made a mistake and let's be honest about it	✓	✓	✓	✓
Supports	We agree that this is a problem that should be addressed – hopefully by someone else	✓	✓	✓	✓
Strengthens	What we said before still hasn't happened and we need to give moral support, if nothing else, to the agency or programme that has to deal with the mess				
Stresses	We really do think this is important and hope someone will listen	✓	✓	✓	✓
Takes into consideration	No one is going to do anything	✓	✓	✓	✓
Urges	We think it is important and someone should do something	✓	✓	✓	✓
Responds warmly	We are thanking someone for doing something	✓	✓	✓	✓
Welcomes	Someone is doing something somewhere	✓	✓	✓	✓

more fraught with possible misunderstandings based on how terms
are understood or translated:

> *Translation, you know, is not a matter of substituting words in
> one language for words in another language. Translation is a
> matter of saying in one language, for a particular situation,
> what a native speaker of the other language would say in the
> same situation. The more unlikely that situation is in one of the
> languages, the harder it is to find a corresponding utterance in
> the other.*
>
> (Suzette Haden Elgin, 1994, *Earthsong*, p9)

In *Pragmatics of Human Communication*, Watzlawick, Beavin and
Jackson (1967) have come up with five axioms:

1   You cannot not communicate.
2   Every interaction has both content and a relationship dimension.
3   Every interaction is defined by the way it is punctuated.
4   Messages are digital and analogical (verbal and non-verbal).
5   Communication exchanges are either symmetrical or
    complementary.

Table 4.1 is an attempt to address, humourously, the key terms used in
negotiations. The design of the table is to give you an idea of the
strength of a term. The table has a horizontal tick box system so that
each term has four levels of strength, starting on the left with the
weakest – just a sentence with the term in it. A combination of the
three possible actions together would, however, give a very strong
message.

MEDIA CAMPAIGNING

A primary goal of NGOs' activities in virtually any UN process is to
increase public awareness of the issues under consideration and the
activities and positions of their own organizations. Gaining media
coverage of such positions by major news organizations can build
pressure on political leaders and influence the positions of
governments during negotiations. It can also build active public
constituencies that support continued action within countries and
regions.

The UN press corps represents a tremendous potential
communications resource. There are over 200 correspondents

regularly covering the UN in New York, from over 120 major newspapers, magazines, television networks and radio stations that serve virtually every country and geographical region. The numbers are similar in Geneva and Vienna. These correspondents are often supplemented by local journalists, freelancers, academics and issue specialists who are assigned to cover stories at major international negotiations.

In New York, the UN journalists' offices are primarily clustered on three floors, in a section of the UN Secretariat and Conference Buildings. This press area is technically restricted to those with UN press credentials, and, as with all things these days, security checks are stricter.

Nevertheless, journalists themselves are usually fairly relaxed about visitors – provided that they are respectful and discrete. This means, for example, that an individual can usually place advisories or press releases in the reporters' post-boxes in New York (on the fourth floor), or go to a scheduled interview with a particular reporter in his or her office. However, roaming the press offices is not advised and posting notices of any type on the walls is definitely not a great idea.

Gaining media coverage at the UN is extremely desirable, and it is possible – but it is not easy. A fast look at the press post-boxes will reveal that each reporter receives 40 or 50 items per day – press releases, advisories, newsletters and background documents. Most of these are competing for the same, very limited, print or broadcast space.

Attempting to reach journalists at the UN should be done with an understanding that although most reporters are not specialists in your field – and therefore require a clear explanation of the issues – their time is extremely limited. Remember, these are the same journalists who are at the UN reporting on issues such as war, peace, drought, refugees and famine. The most important rule is to make sure that your statement identifies issues that are newsworthy and presents them in a clear, focused way.

There are a several useful methods to gain the media's attention.

Media advisories

Announce your event on one page and in only a few words that explain what it is, who is involved and when it is taking place. Identify who is sponsoring the event. Let the press know if credentials are required (for events inside the UN they are; outside press must apply for accreditation from the Department of Public Information in advance).

Press releases

These need to present a clear, focused description of an event or action. A journalist's requirements are very specific. An effective press release should be:

- Complete: it should inform what the activity is, when and where it is happening, who is involved, and why it is significant. It should include some provocative quotes.
- Clearly written: it should explain information in a direct style, much like a news article. It should not sound like a dissertation or a political treatise. It should also not use much scientific, political or technical jargon.
- Concise: two pages should be the most for a press release, written in a readable font (12 point is preferable). The page should be well spaced, without too many fancy graphics. If it needs to have graphs or charts, put them on a background document.

The press release should also provide a contact person. It is very important that you put in a contact name, mobile telephone number, telephone number and email address.

Press conferences

The most comprehensive way to convey a message to the press is, of course, a full news conference. These allow for a broad framing of an issue, statements by expert speakers and direct questions by journalists. Yet, it is often difficult to attract reporters (especially New York reporters) to most NGO press conferences regarding the UN. Reporters from 'outside' of the UN are usually satisfied to repeat their own government's official line, while UN-based reporters, who are often overwhelmed by other major political events, are used to quoting UN and national government officials.

Over the past few years, NGOs active on a variety of issues at the UN have realized that by organizing press conferences and media activities in coalition, they can be far more effective at gaining the press's attention. Press conferences that present speakers from a Northern and Southern NGO, an environmental and a social or development organization, a major NGO and a local one have been able to reach a broader potential journalistic audience.

If these can be held at one of the venues close to the UN press corps offices, they have a far greater chance of succeeding. There are two such venues in New York: the official UN Press Conference Room (S-226) and the lounge of the UN Correspondents Association (UNCA). Each of these requires special permission, or payment of a fee. Both are best organized with the assistance of an experienced media coordinator.

Media coordination for conferences and campaigns

Especially at major conferences and summits, the plethora of NGO voices – all competing for media attention – often have the effect of cancelling each other out. NGOs can be far more effective when presenting their issues to the press as a coalition. The more that leading NGOs can work together on strategies for reaching media, on activities such as press conferences and on their actual positions, the more likely they are to achieve a maximum level of media coverage at meetings.

Making use of an independent media consultant, who is experienced working with international NGOs, can significantly improve media coordination and improve results for coalitions active at an intergovernmental negotiation. Such a consultant can help set up a project to advise NGOs how to promote their positions on policy issues, organize media events, and publicize national and global activities. An effective media project should work with NGOs actively at a conference and at its preparatory meetings. It should be able to cooperate closely with the official conference secretariat and with the UN Department of Public Information (DPI) to obtain optimal access for NGOs to official media facilities and the UN press corps.

Working with NGO coalitions, a media advocacy project can:

- Organize news conferences and background briefings by leading NGOs on active conference issues and on their political status.
- Help produce press releases and media kits covering all issues, from a broad range of international, national and local NGOs.
- Arrange interviews of NGO experts in specific issue areas and from all geographical regions.
- Provide websites, calendars and media advisories.
- Suggest story ideas to journalists and seek cooperation with individual news organizations on coordinating special events.

Chapter 5

How To Get There and Where To Stay

'Would you tell me, please, which way I ought to go from here?'
'That depends a good deal on where you want to get to', said the Cat.
'I don't much care where – ', said Alice.
'Then it doesn't matter which way you go', said the Cat.
' – so long as I get somewhere', Alice added as an explanation.
(Lewis Carroll, *Through the Looking Glass*, 1865)

GETTING AROUND GENEVA AND NEW YORK

From Geneva airport

Geneva airport has excellent transport links into the centre of Geneva. The airport is very close to the city and therefore the time into the centre is around 10 to 20 minutes, depending upon the type of transport you take.

Buses Geneva

Buses Geneva operates an excellent bus system to the city centre from the airport. There are very regular services and the cost is around US$3.

Taxis

These are available at the airport and cost around US$25, including tip, to the centre of Geneva.

Train

There is a station at the airport that will, for US$5, take you into the city centre. Trains go every 10 minutes.

Transportation in Geneva

Taxis

These are relatively expensive. They can be called to your hotel or you may find it possible to hail one on the street. If you are at the UN, it is best to order one.

Buses

These are very regular and a single ticket costs around US$1.50. If you want a 24-hour unlimited ticket, these cost US$6.

From JFK/La Guardia airports

Shuttle buses

Shuttle buses from the major New York airports will take you into Manhattan. From JFK airport, these cost US$13. The bus takes about an hour and arrives at 42nd Street. From La Guardia airport, the cost is US$10. The bus takes about 40 minutes and also stops at 42nd Street.

Taxis

These are also available from the airports but are more expensive. The flat rate from JFK airport to anywhere in Manhattan is US$30 (tolls and tip are extra). From La Guardia airport, it is around US$25.

Subway

It is possible to take the subway from JFK airport. To do this, you take a courtesy bus to the subway station. The subway ride takes about one and a half hours, but only costs US$1.50.

Train Link

This is a new development that takes you directly into Penn Station on the west side of Manhattan at 34th Street. You should allow up to an hour for the journey.

Transportation in Manhattan

Taxis

These are easily hailed on the street. Officially licensed cabs are painted yellow. A light on the roof of the vehicle indicates that the taxi is available for hire.

Subways

Underground trains are a fast means of travel and you can buy multiple tickets if you are going to be in New York for some time. Most of the trains run north–south (up and down Manhattan). Cross-town trains run between Grand Central Station and Times Square on 42nd Street. The cost is US$1.50 irrespective of where you embark or disembark. This buys a token, obtainable from the ticket booth, which is inserted into the turnstile on entrance.

Buses

These are not so fast, although they can be a good way to see New York and there are more cross-town services than on the subway. The fare for a journey of any length is also US$1.50. This is payable as cash (exact change only), token or via Metrocard.

Metrocards

These are the most economical means of paying for subway/bus journeys and one card is valid on both. There are three purchasing options:

1   weekly pass (US$20);
2   one-day pass;
3   single-ride Metrocard, which allows you to load on as much or as little money as you like; a ten-ride card gives you one extra ride free.

Metrocards are available at vending machines, at street-level vendors and at subway ticket booths. On a single journey, so long as you are within a limited time frame, you can transfer to/from one mode to another at no extra cost.

Staying in Geneva and New York

Geneva accommodation[1]

Flats located in the city centre

Residence Cite-Verdaine
Rue du Vieux-Collège 5
Tel: +41 22 312 0120 *or* 317 7120

Residence Dizerens
Rue Dizerens 3
Tel: +41 22 809 5511
www.hotel-swiss.ch
Email:
hotel.dizerens@swissonline.ch

Residence Sagitta
Rue de la Flèche 6
Tel: +41 22 786 3361
www.top-hotels.ch
Email: sagitta@span.ch

Residence Saint-James
Rue Versonnex 3
Tel: +41 22 849 9100
www.st-james.ch
Email: stjames@gic.ch

Residence Studio House Acacias
Route des Acacias 4
Tel: +41 22 304 0300
www.studiohouse.ch
Email: studiohouse@bluewin.ch

Centre for Non-Governmental Organizations and Delegations
Chemin William Rappard 31
Bellevue
Tel: +41 22 959 8855
www.mandint.org
Email: admin@mandint.org

Three-star hotels

Hotel Adriatica
Rue Sautter 21
Tel: +41 22 703 5383
www.hotel-adriatica.com
Email: reservation@hotel-adriatica.com
Situated: Centre/Hospital

Hotel des Alpes
Rue des Alpes 14
Tel: +41 22 731 2200
www.hotel-alpes.ch
Email: info@hotel-alpes.ch
Situated: Gare/Station

Hotel Arcades
Place Cornavin 14–16
Tel: +41 22 732 5948
www.tbh-ge.ch/arcades
Email:
hotel_arcades@hotmail.com
Situated: Gare/Station

Hotel Ascot Manotel
Rue Rothschild 55
Tel: +41 22 544 3838
www.manotel.com
Email: ascot@manotel.com
Situated: Gare/Station

Hotel Astoria
Place Cornavin 6
Tel: +41 22 544 5252
www.astoria-geneve.ch
Email: hotel@astoria-geneve.ch
Situated: Gare/Station

Hotel at Home
Rue de Fribourg 16
Tel: +41 22 906 1900
www.kis.ch/at-home
Email: athome@bluewin.ch
Situated: Gare/Station

Hotel Balzac
Rue de l'Ancien-Port 14
Place de la Navigation
Tel: +41 22 731 0160
www.hotel-balzac.ch
Email: info@hotel-balzac.ch
Situated: Gare/Station

Hotel Calvy
Ruelle du Midi 5
Tel: +41 22 700 2727
www.original.ch/calvy
Email: calvy@bluewin.ch
Situated: Centre/Center

Hotel Capitole
Rue de Berne 15
Tel: +41 22 909 8626
www.hotelcapitole.ch
Email: info@hotelcapitole.com
Situated: Gare/Station

Hotel Carlton
Rue Amat 22
Tel: +41 22 908 6850
Email:
carlton_gva@swissonline.ch
Situated: Gare/Station

Hotel Chantilly Manotel
Rue de la Navigation 27
Tel: +41 22 544 4040
www.manotel.com
Email: chantilly@manotel.com
Situated: Gare/Station

Hotel Comedie
Rue de Carouge 12
Tel: +41 22 322 2324
www.hotel-comedie.ch
Email: info@hotel-comedie.ch
Situated: Centre/Center

Hotel Cristal
Rue Pradier 4
Tel: +41 22 731 3400
www.fhotels.ch
Email: cristal@fhotels.ch
Situated: Gare/Station

Hotel Edelweiss Manotel
Place de la Navigation 2
Tel: +41 22 544 5151
www.manotel.com
Email: edelweiss@manotel.com
Situated: Gare/Station

Auberge du Grand-Saconnex
Route de Ferney 175
Grand-Saconnex
Tel: +41 22 798 0858
www.tbh-ge.ch/grandsac
Email: cvborel@freesurf.ch
Situated: Aéroport/Palexpo/ONU

Hotel le Grenil
Avenue Sainte-Clotilde 7
Tel: +41 22 328 3055
www.grenil.ch
Email: resa@grenil.ch
Situated: Centre/Center

Hotel Moderne
Rue de Berne 1
Tel: +41 22 732 8100
www.hotelmoderne.ch
Email: info@hotelmoderne.ch
Situated: Gare/Station

Hotel Phoenix
Avenue Louis-Casaï 79, Cointrin
Tel: +41 22 710 0303
www.hotel-phoenix.ch
Email: phoenix@capp.ch
Situated: Aéroport/Palexpo

**Hotel Strasbourg et Univers
(Best Western)**
Rue Pradier 10
Tel: +41 22 906 5800
www.strasbourg-geneva.ch
Email: info@hotel-strasbourg-
geneva.ch
Situated: Gare/Station

New York[2]

Here are some suggestions of places in which you might consider staying, based on experiences stakeholders have had over the years. The Manhattan East Suite Hotels, including The Beekman Towers and The Plaza, are where many government officials stay. Remember that for hotels, the price quoted usually excludes local tax; so do ask what the full price is. For flats, tax is generally included.

Big Apple Hostel
119 West 45th Street
Tel: +1 212 302 2603

Hotel Wolcott
4 West 31st Street
Tel: +1 212 268 2900
www.wolcott.com

Iroquois Hotel
49 West 44th Street
Tel: +1 212 840 3080

Manhattan East Suite Hotels
(has ten hotels in New York)
Tel: +1 212 465 3700
www.mesuite.com

**Manhattan Riverside Tower
Hotel**
Tel: +1 800 724 3136

Millennium UN Plaza Hotel
East 44th Street at First Avenue
Tel: +1 212 758 1234
www.millennium-hotel.org

Pickwick Arms Hotel
230 East 51st Street
Tel: +1 212 355 0300

Roger Smith Hotel
501 Lexington Avenue
(corner of 48th Street)
Tel: +1 212 755 1400

Vanderbilt YMCA
224 East 47th Street
Tel: +1 212 756 9600

Web resources

New York Hotel Discounts and City Guide
www.worldexecutive.com/
cityguides/new_york
Comprehensive list of hotels arranged by price. Each listing has telephone and fax numbers, and several include prices on rooms or suites.

New York Accommodations Online
www.newyorkhotelsonline.com/
save/newyork-save
Discounted reservations

Priceline.com
www.priceline.com
Name your own price for airline tickets, hotel rooms and more!

New York City Hotel Reservations, Discounts, Savings, Deals
www.express-res.com

Discount New York City Hotel Reservations
www.hotres.com

Hotel Hotline in New York
www.hoteldiscount.com
130 hotels from US$69 a night

Chapter 6

Important Information

Never look down on anybody unless you're helping him up.
(Jesse Jackson)[1]

PERMANENT MISSIONS TO THE UN IN GENEVA AND NEW YORK

Geneva, Switzerland[2]

Afghanistan
Permanent Representative of the Islamic State of Afghanistan to the United Nations
Rue de Lausanne 63 (5ième étage), 1202 Genève
Tel: +41 22 731 1616 •
Fax: +41 22 731 4510

Albania
Permanent Representative of the Republic of Albania to the United Nations
Rue du Môle 32 (Apt 12), 1201 Genève
Tel: +41 22 731 1143 •
Fax: +41 22 738 8156
Email: albaniemiss@bluewin.ch

Algeria
Permanent Representative of Algeria to the United Nations
Route de Lausanne 308, 1293 Bellevue, Genève
Tel: +41 22 774 1985/1986 •
Fax: +41 22 774 3049

Andorra
Permanent Representative of the Principality of Andorra to the United Nations
Rue de Chantepoulet 1–3 (7ième étage), 1201 Genève

Angola
Permanent Representative of the Republic of Angola to the United Nations
Rue de Lausanne 45–47, 1201

Genève
Tel: +41 22 732 3060 •
Fax: +41 22 732 3084
Email: mission.angola@itu.ch

Antigua and Barbuda

Permanent Representative of
Antigua and Barbuda to the
United Nations
15 Thayer Street, London, W1M
5LD, UK
Tel: +44 20 7486 7073 •
Fax: +44 20 7486 9970

Argentina

Permanent Representative of
Argentina to the United Nations
Route de l'Aéroport 10
PO Box 536, 1215 Genève 15
Tel: +41 22 929 8600 •
Fax: +41 22 798 5995/1992

Armenia

Permanent Representative of the
Republic of Armenia to the
United Nations
Avenue du Mail 28, 1205 Genève
Tel: +41 22 320 1100 •
Fax: +41 22 320 1112

Australia

Permanent Representative of
Australia to the United Nations
Rue de Moillebeau 56, 1209
Genève
PO Box 172, 1211 Genève 19
Tel: +41 22 918 2900 •
Fax: +41 22 733 6586

Austria

Permanent Representative of
Austria to the United Nations

Rue de Varembé 9–11
PO Box 68, 1211 Genève 20
Tel: +41 22 748 2048 •
Fax: +41 22 748 2040
Email: mission.austria@itu.ch

Azerbaijan

Permanent Representative of the
Republic of Azerbaijan to the
United Nations
Rue de Lausanne 67, 1202
Genève
Tel: +41 22 901 1815 •
Fax: +41 22 901 1844

Bahrain

Permanent Representative of the
State of Bahrain to the United
Nations
Chemin William Barbey 51
PO Box 39, 1292 Chambésy
Tel: +41 22 758 2102/2103 •
Fax: +41 22 758 1310

Bangladesh

Permanent Representative of the
People's Republic of Bangladesh
to the United Nations
Rue de Lausanne 65, 1202
Genève
Tel: +41 22 906 8020 •
Fax: +41 22 738 4616
Email:
bangla.perm@ge.maxess.ch

Barbados

Permanent Representative of
Barbados to the United Nations
Avenue Général Latrigue 78,
1200 Bruxelles, Belgium
Tel: +32 2 732 1737/1867 •
Fax: +32 2 732 3266

Belarus
Permanent Representative of the
Republic of Belarus to the United
Nations
Avenue de la Paix 15, 1211
Genève 20
Tel: +41 22 734 3844 •
Fax: +41 22 734 3844

Belgium
Permanent Representative of
Belgium to the United Nations
Rue de Moillebeau 58 (6ième
étage)
PO Box 473, 1211 Genève 19
Tel +41 22 730 4000 •
Fax: +41 22 734 5079
Email: mission.belgium@itu.ch

Belize
Permanent Representative of
Belize to the United Nations
Rue de Mont-Blanc 7 (5ième
étage), 1201 Genève
Tel: +41 22 906 8420 •
Fax: +41 22 906 8429
Email:
mission.belize@ties.itu.int

Benin
Permanent Representative of the
Republic of Benin to the United
Nations
Avenue de l'Observatoire 5,
1180 Bruxelles, Belgium
Tel: +32 2 374 9192 or 375 0674 •
Fax: +32 2 375 8326

Bhutan
Permanent Representative of the
Kingdom of Bhutan to the
United Nations

Chemin du Champ-d'Anier
17–19, 1209 Genève
Tel: +41 22 799 0890 •
Fax: +41 22 799 0899

Bolivia
Permanent Representative of
Bolivia to the United Nations
Rue du Valais 7 bis, 1202 Genève
Tel: +41 22 731 2725/3096 •
Fax: +41 22 738 0222
Email: mission.bolivia@itu.ch

Bosnia and Herzegovina
Permanent Representative of the
Republic of Bosnia and
Herzegovina to the United
Nations
Rue Lamartine 22 bis, 1203
Genève
Tel: +41 22 345 8844/8858 •
Fax: +41 22 345 8889

Botswana
Permanent Representative of
Botswana to the United Nations
Rue de Lausanne 80, 1201
Genève

Brazil
Permanent Representative of
Brazil to the United Nations
Ancienne Route 17B, 1218
Grand-Saconnex
Tel: +41 22 929 0900 •
Fax: +41 22 788 2505/2506
Email: mission.brazil@itu.ch

Brunei Darussalam
Permanent Representative of
Brunei Darussalam to the United
Nations

International Center Cointrin (ICC), Bloc F/G, 5ième étage, Route de Pré-Bois 20
PO Box 1806, 1215 Genève 15
Tel: +41 22 929 8240 •
Fax: +41 22 788 5230

Bulgaria
Permanent Representative of the Republic of Bulgaria to the United Nations
Chemin des Crêts-de-Pregny 16, 1218 Grand-Saconnex
Tel: +41 22 798 0300/0301 •
Fax: +41 22 798 0302

Burundi
Permanent Representative of the Republic of Burundi to the United Nations
Rue du Fort-Barreau 13, 1201 Genève
Tel: +41 22 734 8000 •
Fax: +41 22 774 1019

Cambodia
Permanent Representative of the Kingdom of Cambodia to the United Nations
Rue Adolphe Yvon 4, 75116 Paris, France
Tel: +33 1 4503 4720 •
Fax: +33 1 4503 4740

Cameroon
Permanent Representative of the Republic of Cameroon to the United Nations
Rue du Nant 6–8, 1207 Genève
Tel: +41 22 736 2022 *or* 787 5040 •
Fax: +41 22 736 2165

Canada
Permanent Representative of Canada to the United Nations
Rue du Pré-de-la-Bichette 1, 1202 Genève
Tel: +41 22 919 9200 •
Fax: +41 22 919 9227

Cape Verde
Permanent Representative of the Republic of Cape Verde to the United Nations
Avenue Blanc 47
PO Box 80, 1211 Genève 25
Tel: +41 22 733 3336 •
Fax: +41 22 731 3540

Central African Republic
Permanent Representative of the Central African Republic to the United Nations
Route de Colovrex 16
PO Box 115, 1218 Grand-Saconnex
Tel: +41 22 920 6000 •
Fax: +41 22 920 6001

Chile
Permanent Representative of Chile to the United Nations
Rue de Moillebeau 58 (4ième étage)
PO Box 332, 1211 Genève 19
Tel: +41 22 919 8800 •
Fax: +41 22 734 5297

China
Permanent Representative of the People's Republic of China to the United Nations
Chemin de Surville 11
PO Box 85, 1213 Petit-Lancy 2

Tel: +41 22 792 2548/2543 *or*
793 3591 •
Fax: +41 22 793 7014
Email: mission.china@itu.ch

Colombia
Permanent Representative of
Colombia to the United Nations
Chemin du Champ-d'Anier
17–19, 1209 Genève
Tel: +41 22 798 4554/4555 •
Fax: +41 22 791 0787

Congo
Permanent Representative of the
Republic of the Congo to the
United Nations
Chemin de Thury 2, 1206 Genève
Tel: +41 22 346 6124 •
Fax: +41 22 346 6192

Costa Rica
Permanent Representative of
Costa Rica to the United Nations
Rue de Butini 11, 1202 Genève
Tel: +41 22 731 2587 •
Fax: +41 22 731 2069
Email:
mission.costa-rica@itu.ch

Côte d'Ivoire
Permanent Representative of
Côte d'Ivoire to the United
Nations
Route de Ferney 149H
PO Box 315, 1218 Grand-
Saconnex
Tel: +41 22 717 0250 •
Fax: +41 22 717 0260
Email:
mission.ccte-divoire@itu.ch

Croatia
Permanent Representative of the
Republic of Croatia to the United
Nations
Route de Ferney 25, 1202
Genève
Tel: +41 22 740 3243/3244 •
Fax: +41 22 740 3251
Email: croatia@ties.itu.ch

Cuba
Permanent Representative of
Cuba to the United Nations
Chemin de Valérie 100, 1292
Chambésy
Tel: +41 22 758 9430 •
Fax: +41 22 758 9431
Email: mission-cuba@itu.ch *or*
mission-cuba.oficomex@itu.ch

Cyprus
Permanent Representative of
Cyprus to the United Nations
Chemin François-Lehmann 34
(7ième étage)
PO Box 113, 1218 Grand-
Saconnex
Tel: +41 22 798 2150/2175 •
Fax: +41 22 791 0084

Czech Republic
Permanent Representative of the
Czech Republic to the United
Nations
Chemin Louis Dunant 17
PO Box 109, 1211 Genève 20
Tel: +41 22 740 3888/3668/3661 •
Fax: +41 22 740 3662
Email: mission.czgeneva@itu.ch

Democratic People's Republic of Korea

Permanent Representative of the Democratic People's Republic of Korea to the United Nations
Chemin de Plonjon 1, 1207 Genève
Tel: +41 22 735 4370 •
Fax: +41 22 786 0662

Democratic Republic of the Congo

Permanent Representative of the Democratic Republic of the Congo to the United Nations
Avenue de Budé 18 (Local 1822), 1202 Genève
PO Box 2595, 1211 Genève 2
Tel: +41 22 740 3744 •
Fax: +41 22 740 3744

Denmark

Permanent Representative of Denmark to the United Nations
Rue de Moillebeau 56 (7ième étage)
PO Box 435, 1211 Genève 19
Tel: +41 22 918 0040 •
Fax: +41 22 918 0066
Email: mission.denmark@itu.ch

Dominica

Permanent Representative of the Commonwealth of Dominica to the United Nations
1 Colingham Gardens, Earls Court, London, SW5 0HW, UK
Tel: +44 20 7370 5194/5195 •
Fax: +44 20 7373 8743
Email: geninfo@dominica.co.uk

Dominican Republic

Permanent Representative of the Dominican Republic to the United Nations
Rue de Lausanne 65 (2ième étage), 1202 Genève
Tel: +41 22 731 3079 •
Fax: +41 22 741 0590

Ecuador

Permanent Representative of Ecuador to the United Nations
Rue de Lausanne 145 (7ième étage), 1202 Genève
Tel: +41 22 731 4879/5289 •
Fax: +41 22 738 2676

Egypt

Permanent Representative of the Arab Republic of Egypt to the United Nations
Avenue Blanc 49 (2ième étage), 1202 Genève
Tel: +41 22 731 6530/6539/2638 •
Fax: +41 22 738 4415

El Salvador

Permanent Representative of El Salvador to the United Nations
Rue de Lausanne 65 (2ième étage), 1202 Genève
Tel: +41 22 732 7036 •
Fax: +41 22 738 4744
Email: 75363,1247@compuserve.com

Eritrea

Permanent Representative of Eritrea to the United Nations
9 rue du Vermont
PO Box 85, 1211 Genève 20
Tel: +41 22 740 2840 •
Fax: +41 22 740 4949

Estonia
Permanent Representative of the
Republic of Estonia to the United
Nations
Chemin du Petit-Saconnex 28a,
1209 Genève
PO Box 358, 1211 Genève 19
Tel: +41 22 919 1980 •
Fax: +41 22 919 1981

Ethiopia
Permanent Representative of the
Federal Democratic Republic of
Ethiopia to the United Nations
Rue de Moillebeau 56
PO Box 338, 1211 Genève 19
Tel: +41 22 919 7010 •
Fax: +41 22 919 7029
Email: mission.ethiopia@itu.ch

Finland
Permanent Representative of
Finland to the United Nations
Rue Pré-de-la-Bichette 1
PO Box 198, 1211 Genève 20
Tel: +41 22 919 4242 •
Fax: +41 22 740 0287

**Former Yugoslav Republic of
Macedonia**
Permanent Representative of the
Former Yugoslav Republic of
Macedonia
Rue de Lausanne 143, 1202
Genève
Tel: +41 22 731 2930 •
Fax: +41 22 731 2939

France
Permanent Representative of
France to the United Nations
Villa 'Les Ormeaux', Route de

Pregny 36, 1292 Chambésy
Tel: +41 22 758 9111 •
Fax: +41 22 758 9137/2449

Gabon
Permanent Representative of the
Gabonese Republic to the United
Nations
Avenue Blanc 47
PO Box 12, 1211 Genève 7
Tel: +41 22 731 6869/6847 •
Fax: +41 22 731 6866

Gambia
Permanent Representative of the
Gambia to the United Nations
Rue du Rhône 30, 1204 Genève
Tel: +41 22 312 4347 •
Fax: +41 22 312 4358

Georgia
Permanent Representative of
Georgia to the United Nations
Rue Richard Wagner 1 (6ième
étage), 1202 Genève
Tel: +41 22 919 1010/1017 •
Fax: +41 22 733 9033

Germany
Permanent Representative of
Germany to the United Nations
Chemin du Petit-Saconnex 28C,
1209 Genève
PO Box 171, 1211 Genève 19
Tel: +41 22 730 1111 •
Fax: +41 22 734 3043
Email: mission.germany@itu.ch

Ghana
Permanent Representative of
Ghana to the United Nations
Rue de Moillebeau 56, 1209

Genève
Tel: +41 22 919 0450/0452 •
Fax: +41 22 734 9161

Greece

Permanent Representative of
Greece to the United Nations
Place Saint-Gervais 1, 1201
Genève
Tel: +41 22 732 3356/3357 •
Fax: +41 22 732 2150

Grenada

Permanent Representative of
Grenada to the United Nations
Bureaux 40 et 41, Avenue Luis
Casai 18, 1228 Genève 28
Tel: +41 22 747 7741 •
Fax: +41 22 747 7914

Guatemala

Permanent Representative of
Guatemala to the United Nations
Chemin de Sous-Bois 21
1202 Genève
Tel: +41 22 734 5573 *or* 733 0850 •
Fax: +41 22 733 1429
Email:
mission.guatemala@itu.ch

Guinea

Permanent Representative of the
Republic of Guinea to the United
Nations
Rue du Valais 7–9, 1202 Genève
Tel: +41 22 731 6555 •
Fax: +41 22 731 6554
Email:
mission.guinea@ties.itu.ch

Guinea-Bissau

Permanent Representative of the
Republic of Guinea-Bissau to the
United Nations
Avenue Franklin Roosevelt 70
1050 Bruxelles, Belgique
Tel: +32 2 647 0890/1351 •
Fax: +32 2 640 4312

Haiti

Permanent Representative of
Haiti to the United Nations
Rue de Monthoux 64, 1201
Genève
Tel: +41 22 732 7628 •
Fax: +41 22 732 5536

Honduras

Permanent Representative of
Honduras to the United Nations
Chemin de Taverney 13, 1218
Grand-Saconnex
Tel: +41 22 710 0760 •
Fax: +41 22 710 0766
Email: mission.honduras-
onu@itu.ch

Hungary

Permanent Representative of the
Republic of Hungary to the
United Nations
Avenue de Champel 81, 1206
Genève
Tel: +41 22 346 0323/5165 or
347 9147 •
Fax: +41 22 346 5861
Email: mission.hungary@itu.ch

Iceland

Permanent Representative of
Iceland to the United Nations
Avenue Blanc 49

PO Box 86, 1211 Genève 20
Tel: +41 22 716 1700 •
Fax: +41 22 716 1707

India

Permanent Representative of
India to the United Nations
Rue du Valais 9 (6ième étage),
1202 Genève
Tel: +41 22 732 0859 •
Fax: +41 22 731 5471 or 738 4548

Indonesia

Permanent Representative of the
Republic of Indonesia to the
United Nations
Rue de Saint-Jean 16, 1203
Genève
PO Box 2271, 1211 Genève 2
Tel: +41 22 345 3350 •
Fax: +41 22 345 5733

Iran (Islamic Republic of)

Permanent Representative of the
Islamic Republic of Iran to the
United Nations
Chemin du Petit-Saconnex 28,
1209 Genève
Tel: +41 22 733 3001/3004 •
Fax: +41 22 733 0203

Iraq

Permanent Representative of
Iraq to the United Nations
Chemin du Petit-Saconnex 28A,
1209 Genève
Tel: +41 22 918 0980 •
Fax: +41 22 733 0326

Ireland

Permanent Representative of
Ireland to the United Nations
Rue de Moillebeau 58 (8ième
étage)
PO Box 2566, 1209 Genève (non
pas 1211 Genève 19)
Tel: +41 22 732 8550 •
Fax: +41 22 732 8106 or 731
4365
Email: pmungeneva.ireland@
iveagh.irlgov.ie

Israel

Permanent Representative of
Israel to the United Nations
Avenue de la Paix 1–3, 1202
Genève
Tel: +41 22 716 0500 •
Fax: +41 22 716 0555
Email: mission.israel@itu.ch

Italy

Permanent Representative of
Italy to the United Nations
Chemin de l'Impératrice 10,
1292 Pregny
Tel: +41 22 918 0810 •
Fax: +41 22 734 6702 or 733
0783
Email: mission.italy@itu.ch

Jamaica

Permanent Representative of
Jamaica
Rue de Lausanne 36, 1201
Genève
Tel: +41 22 731 5780 •
Fax: +41 22 738 4420

Japan

Permanent Representative of
Japan to the United Nations
Chemin des Fins 3
PO Box 337, 1211 Genève 19

Tel: +41 22 717 3111 •
Fax: +41 22 788 3811

Jordan
Permanent Representative of the
Hashemite Kingdom of Jordan to
the United Nations
Rue de Lausanne 45–47
PO Box 1716, 1211 Genève 1
Tel: +41 22 731 7134/7135 •
Fax: +41 22 738 5841

Kazakhstan
Permanent Representative of the
Republic of Kazakhstan to the
United Nations
Chemin de Prunier 10
PO Box 6, 1218 Grand-Saconnex
Tel: +41 22 788 6660 •
Fax: +41 22 788 6602

Kenya
Permanent Representative of the
Republic of Kenya to the United
Nations
Avenue de la Paix 1–3 (1ère
étage), 1202 Genève
Tel: +41 22 906 4050 •
Fax: +41 22 731 2905

Kuwait
Permanent Representative of the
State of Kuwait to the United
Nations
Avenue de l'Ariana 2, 1202
Genève
Tel: +41 22 918 0100 •
Fax: +41 22 740 2155 or 918 0148
Email: mission.kuwait@itu.ch

Kyrgyzstan
Permanent Representative of the
Kyrgyz Republic to the United

Nations
Rue Manoir 26, 1207 Genève
Tel: +41 22 707 9220 •
Fax: +41 22 707 9221
Email: mission.kyrgyzstan@itu.ch

Latvia
Permanent Representative of the
Republic of Latvia to the United
Nations
Rue de Lausanne 137 (6ième
étage)
PO Box 193, 1211 Genève 20
Tel: +41 22 738 5111 •
Fax: +41 22 738 5171
Email:
romans.baumanis@span.ch

Lebanon
Permanent Representative of
Lebanon to the United Nations
Parc des Mayens 28, 1218
Grand-Saconnex
Tel: +41 22 791 8585 •
Fax: +41 22 791 8580

Lesotho
Permanent Representative of the
Kingdom of Lesotho to the
United Nations
Rue de Lausanne 44 (1ère
étage), 1201 Genève
Tel: +41 22 900 0505 •
Fax: +41 22 900 0525

Libyan Arab Jamahiriya
Permanent Representative of the
Socialist People's Libyan Arab
Jamahiriya to the United Nations
Chemin de Champ-Vovan 10,
1294 Genthod
Tel: +41 22 774 3073 •
Fax: +41 22 774 3073

Liechtenstein
Permanent Representative of the Principality of Liechtenstein to the United Nations
Rue de Montbrillant 54–56, 1202 Genève
PO Box 158, 1211 Genève 20
Tel: +41 22 734 2900 •
Fax: +41 22 734 2951

Lithuania
Permanent Representative of the Republic of Lithuania to the United Nations
Avenue du Bouchet 18, 1209 Genève
Tel: +41 22 734 5101 •
Fax: +41 22 734 5070
Email: lt.mission.geneva@bluewin.ch

Luxembourg
Permanent Representative of Luxembourg to the United Nations
Chemin de la Rochette (4ième étage), 1202 Genève
Tel: +41 22 919 1929 •
Fax: +41 22 919 1920
Email: mission.luxembourg@ties.itu.int

Madagascar
Permanent Representative of the Republic of Madagascar to the United Nations
Avenue Riant-Parc 32, 1209 Genève
Tel: +41 22 740 1650/2714 •
Fax: +41 22 740 1616

Malaysia
Permanent Representative of Malaysia to the United Nations
International Centre Cointrin (ICC), 1ère étage – bloc H, Route de Pré-Bois 20
PO Box 18341, 1215 Genève 15
Tel: +41 22 788 1505/1509/1523 •
Fax: +41 22 788 0492
Email: mission.malaysia@itu.ch

Mali
Permanent Representative of the Republic of Mali to the United Nations
Basteistrasse 86, 53173 Bonn, Allemagne, Germany
Tel: +49 22 835 7048 •
Fax: +49 22 836 1922

Malta
Permanent Representative of Malta to the United Nations
Parc du Château-Banquet 26, 1202 Genève
Tel: +41 22 901 0580 •
Fax: +41 22 738 1120
Email: mission.malta-gva@itu.ch

Mauritania
Permanent Representative of the Islamic Republic of Mauritania to the United Nations
Avenue Blanc 46, 1202 Genève
Tel: +41 22 906 1840 •
Fax: +41 22 906 1841

Mauritius
Permanent Representative of the Republic of Mauritius to the United Nations

Chemin Louis-Dunant 7–9, 1202
Genève
Tel: +41 22 734 8550 •
Fax: +41 22 734 8630

Mexico
Permanent Representative of
Mexico to the United Nations
Avenue de Budé 16 (7ième
étage), 1202 Genève
PO Box 433, 1211 Genève 19
Tel: +41 22 748 0707 •
Fax: +41 22 748 0708
Email:
mission.mexico@ties.itu.int

Mongolia
Permanent Representative of
Mongolia to the United Nations
Chemin des Mollies 4, 1293
Bellevue
Tel: +41 22 774 1974/1975 •
Fax: +41 22 774 3201
Email:mission.mongolia@itu.ch

Monaco
Permanent Representative of
Monaco to the United Nations
56 rue de Moillebeau, 1209
Genève
Tel: +41 22 919 046 •
Fax: +41 22 919 0469

Morocco
Permanent Representative of the
Kingdom of Morocco to the
United Nations
Chemin François-Lehmann 18A
PO Box 244, 1218 Grand-
Saconnex
Tel: +41 22 798 1535/1536 •
Fax: +41 22 798 4702

Mozambique
Permanent Representative of the
Republic of Mozambique to the
United Nations
Rue Gautier 13 (1ère étage),
1201 Genève
Tel: +41 22 901 1783 •
Fax: +41 22 901 1784

Myanmar
Permanent Representative of the
Union of Myanmar to the United
Nations
Avenue Blanc 47, 1202 Genève
Tel: +41 22 731 7540/7549 •
Fax: +41 22 738 4882
Email: mission.myanmar@itu.ch

Nepal
Permanent Representative of the
Kingdom of Nepal to the United
Nations
Rue de la Servette 81, 1201
Genève
Tel: +41 22 733 2600/2621 •
Fax: +41 22 733 2722

The Netherlands
Permanent Representative of the
Kingdom of The Netherlands to
the United Nations
Chemin des Anémones 11,
Genève
PO Box 276, 1219 Châtelaine
Tel: +41 22 795 1500 •
Fax: +41 22 795 1515

New Zealand
Permanent Representative of
New Zealand to the United
Nations
Chemin du Petit-Saconnex 28a

PO Box 334, 1211 Genève 19
Tel: +41 22 734 9530 •
Fax: +41 22 734 3062

Nicaragua
Permanent Representative of
Nicaragua to the United Nations
Rue du Roveray 16, 1207
Genève
Tel: +41 22 737 3090 •
Fax: +41 22 736 6012
Email: mission.nicaragua@itu.ch

Niger
Permanent Representative of the
Niger to the United Nations
Avenue Franklin Roosevelt 78,
1050 Bruxelles, Belgique
Tel: +32 2 648 6140 •
Fax: +32 2 648 2784

Nigeria
Permanent Representative of
Nigeria to the United Nations
Rue Richard Wagner 1, 1211
Genève 2
Tel: +41 22 730 1414/1415/1416 •
Fax: +41 22 734 1053
Email:
nigeriagva@atge.automail.com

Norway
Permanent Representative of
Norway to the United Nations
Avenue de Budé 35
PO Box 274, 1211 Genève 19
Tel: +41 22 918 0400 •
Fax: +41 22 918 0410/0411

Oman
Permanent Representative of the
Sultanate of Oman to the United

Nations
Chemin du Petit-Saconnex 28b
(entrée C), 1209 Genève
Tel: +41 22 733 7320/7329 *or*
734 1453 •
Fax: +41 22 740 1075
Email:mission.oman@itu.ch

Pakistan
Permanent Representative of
Pakistan to the United Nations
Rue de Moillebeau 56 (4ième
étage)
PO Box 434, 1211 Genève 19
Tel: +41 22 734 7760 •
Fax: +41 22 734 8085
Email: pakistan@itu.ch

Panama
Permanent Representative of
Panama to the United Nations
Rue de Lausanne 72, 1202
Genève
Tel: +41 22 715 0450 •
Fax: +41 22 738 0363
Email: mission.panama@itu.ch

Paraguay
Permanent Representative of
Paraguay to the United Nations
Chemin du Petit-Saconnex 28a,
1209 Genève
Tel: +41 22 740 3211/3213 •
Fax: +41 22 740 3290
Email: mission.paraguay@itu.ch

Peru
Permanent Representative of
Peru to the United Nations
Avenue Louis Casai 71, Genève
PO Box 160, 1216 Cointrin,
Genève

Tel: +41 22 791 7720 •
Fax: +41 22 791 7728/7729
Email: mission.peru@itu.ch

Philippines
Permanent Representative of the
Republic of the Philippines to
the United Nations
Avenue Blanc 47, 1202 Genève
Tel: +41 22 716 1930/1933/1939 •
Fax: +41 22 716 1932
Email:
philippine.mission@itu.ch

Poland
Permanent Representative of the
Republic of Poland to the United
Nations
Chemin de l'Ancienne Route 15
PO Box 126, 1218 Grand-
Saconnex
Tel: +41 22 798 1161/1162/1170 •
Fax: +41 22 798 1175

Portugal
Permanent Representative of
Portugal to the United Nations
PO Box 51, 1211 Genève 20
Tel: +41 22 918 0200 •
Fax: +41 22 918 0228
Email: mission.portugal@itu.ch

Qatar
Permanent Representative of the
State of Qatar to the United
Nations
Route de Ferney 149b, 1218
Grand-Saconnex
Tel: +41 22 798 8500/8501 •
Fax: +41 22 791 0485

Republic of Korea
Permanent Representative of the
Republic of Korea to the United
Nations
Avenue de l'Ariana 1
PO Box 42, 1211 Genève 20
Tel: +41 22 748 0000 •
Fax: +41 22 748 0001

Republic of Moldova
Permanent Representative of the
Republic of Moldova to the
United Nations
Chemin du Régiment-de-Conti
14, 1290 Versoix
Tel: +41 22 755 1890/1891 •
Fax: +41 22 755 1880

Romania
Permanent Representative of
Romania to the United Nations
Chemin de la Perrière 6, 1223
Cologny
Tel: +41 22 752 1090/5555 •
Fax: +41 22 752 2976

Russian Federation
Permanent Representative of the
Russian Federation to the United
Nations
Avenue de la Paix 15
PO Box, 1211 Genève 20
Tel: +41 22 733 1870 or 734
6630/4618 •
Fax: +41 22 734 4044

Rwanda
Permanent Representative of the
Rwandese Republic to the United
Nations
Rue de la Servette 93, 1202
Genève

Tel: +41 22 919 1000 •
Fax: +41 22 919 1001

San Marino
Permanent Representative of the
Republic of San Marino to the
United Nations
Rue de la Faucille 14, 1201
Genève
Tel: +41 22 918 5020 *or* 740 1231 •
Fax: +41 22 918 5030

Saudi Arabia
Permanent Representative of
Saudi Arabia to the United
Nations
Route de Lausanne 263, 1292
Chambésy
Tel: +41 22 758 2441 •
Fax: +41 22 758 0000

Senegal
Permanent Representative of the
Republic of Senegal to the
United Nations
Rue de la Servette 93, 1202
Genève
Tel: +41 22 918 0230 •
Fax: +41 22 740 0711

Singapore
Permanent Representative of the
Republic of Singapore to the
United Nations
Route de Pré-Bois 20, ICC, Bloc
G (6ième étage)
PO Box 1910, 1215 Genève 15
Tel: +41 22 929 6655 •
Fax: +41 22 929 6658
Email: singpmg@planet.ch

Slovakia
Permanent Representative of the
Slovak Republic to the United
Nations
Chemin de l'Ancienne Route 9
PO Box 160, 1218 Grand-
Saconnex
Tel: +41 22 798 9181/9182 •
Fax: +41 22 788 0919

Slovenia
Permanent Representative of
Slovenia to the United Nations
Rue de Lausanne 147, 1202
Genève
Tel: +41 22 738 6660 •
Fax: +41 22 738 6665

Somalia
Permanent Representative of the
Somali Republic to the United
Nations
Rue du Valais 9, 1202 Genève
Tel: +41 22 731 5450 •
Fax: 41 22 798 0732

South Africa
Permanent Representative of the
Republic of South Africa to the
United Nations
Rue du Rhône 65, 1204 Genève
Tel: +41 22 849 5454 •
Fax: +41 22 849 5432

Spain
Permanent Representative of
Spain to the United Nations
Avenue Blanc 53, 1202 Genève
PO Box 201, 1211 Genève 20
Tel: +41 22 731 22 30 *or*
732 9930 •
Fax: +41 22 731 5370

Sri Lanka
Permanent Representative of the
Democratic Socialist Republic of
Sri Lanka to the United Nations
Rue de Moillebeau 56 (5ième
étage)
PO Box 436, 1211 Genève 19
Tel: +41 22 919 1250 •
Fax: +41 22 734 9084

Sudan
Permanent Representative of the
Republic of the Sudan to the
United Nations
Avenue Blanc 49, 1202 Genève
PO Box 335, 1211 Genève 19
Tel: +41 22 731 2663/2666 •
Fax: +41 22 731 2656

Sweden
Permanent Representative of
Sweden to the United Nations
Rue de Lausanne 82, 1202
Genève
PO Box 190, 1211 Genève 20
Tel: +41 22 908 0800 •
Fax: +41 22 908 0810

Switzerland
Permanent Representative of
Switzerland to the United
Nations
Rue de Varembé 9/11, 1211
Genève 20
Tel: +41 22 749 2424 •
Fax: +41 22 749 2437

Syrian Arab Republic
Permanent Representative of the
Syrian Arab Republic to the
United Nations
Rue de Lausanne 72 (3ième

étage), 1202 Genève
Tel: +41 22 732 6522/6626 •
Fax: +41 22 738 4275

Thailand
Permanent Representative of
Thailand to the United Nations
Chemin du Petit-Saconnex 28b,
1209 Genève
Tel: +41 22 734 2010/2018/2020 •
Fax: +41 22 733 3678

Togo
Permanent Representative of
Togo to the United Nations
Rue Alfred Roll 8, 75017 Paris,
France
Tel: +33 14 380 1213 •
Fax: +33 14 380 9071

Trinidad and Tobago
Permanent Representative of the
Republic of Trinidad and Tobago
to the United Nations
Rue de Vermont 37–39, 1211
Genève 20
Tel: +41 22 918 0380 •
Fax: +41 22 734 9138
Email: mission.trinidad-
tobago@itu.ch

Tunisia
Permanent Representative of
Tunisia to the United Nations
Rue de Moillebeau 58, Genève
PO Box 272, 1211 Genève 19
Tel: +41 22 734 8450/8459 •
Fax: +41 22 734 0663

Turkey
Permanent Representative of
Turkey to the United Nations

Chemin du Petit-Saconnex 28B,
Genève
PO Box 371, 1211 Genève 19
Tel: +41 22 918 5080 •
Fax: +41 22 734 0859/5209
Email: mission.turkey@itu.ch

Uganda
Permanent Representative of the
Republic of Uganda to the
United Nations
Rue Antoine Carteret 6 bis, 1202
Genève
Tel: +41 22 339 8810 •
Fax: +41 22 340 3525
Email: mission.uganda@itu.int

Ukraine
Permanent Representative of
Ukraine to the United Nations
Rue de l'Orangerie 14, 1202
Genève
Tel: +41 22 740 3270 •
Fax: +41 22 734 3801

United Arab Emirates
Permanent Representative of the
United Arab Emirates to the
United Nations
Rue de Moillebeau 58, 1209
Genève
Tel: +41 22 918 0000 •
Fax: +41 22 734 5562

**United Kingdom of Great
Britain and Northern Ireland**
Permanent Representative of the
United Kingdom to the United
Nations
Rue de Vermont 37–39, 1211
Genève 20
PO Box, 1211 Genève 20

Tel: +41 22 918 2300 •
Fax: +41 22 918 2333
Email: mission.uk@itu.ch

United Republic of Tanzania
Permanent Representative of the
United Republic of Tanzania to
the United Nations
Avenue Blanc 47, 1202 Genève
Tel: +41 22 731 8920 •
Fax: +41 22 732 8255
Email: mission.tanzania@itu.ch

United States of America
Permanent Representative of the
United States to the United
Nations
Route de Pregny 11, 1292
Chambésy
Tel: +41 22 749 4111 •
Fax: +41 22 749 4880

Uruguay
Permanent Representative of
Uruguay to the United Nations
Rue de Lausanne 65 (4ième
étage), 1202 Genève
Tel: +41 22 732 8366 •
Fax: +41 22 731 5650
Email: mission.uruguay@itu.ch

Venezuela
Permanent Representative of
Venezuela to the United Nations
Chemin François-Lehmann 18A
PO Box 144, 1218 Grand-
Saconnex
Tel: +41 22 798
2621/2622/2623/2058/2065 •
Fax: +41 22 798 5877

Viet Nam
Permanent Representative of the
Socialist Republic of Viet Nam to
the United Nations
Chemin François-Lehmann 18A
(1ère étage), 1218 Grand-
Saconnex
Tel: +41 22 798 2485 •
Fax: +41 22 798 0724

Yemen
Permanent Representative of the
Republic of Yemen to the United
Nations
Chemin du Jonc 19, 1216
Cointrin
Tel: +41 22 799 0510 •
Fax: +41 22 798 0465
Email: yemen@ties.itu.ch

Yugoslavia
Permanent Representative of the
Federal Republic of Yugoslavia to
the United Nations
Chemin Thury 5, 1206 Genève
Tel: +41 22 839 3344 •
Fax: +41 22 839 3359

Zambia
Permanent Representative of the
Republic of Zambia to the United
Nations
Chemin du Champ-d'Anier
17–19, 1209 Genève
Tel: +41 22 788 5330/5331 •
Fax: +41 22 788 5340

Zimbabwe
Permanent Representative of the
Republic of Zimbabwe to the
United Nations
Chemin William Barbey 27, 1292

Chambésy
Tel: +41 22 758 3011/3013/3026 •
Fax: +41 22 758 3044

New York[3]

Afghanistan
Permanent Representative of the
Islamic State of Afghanistan to
the United Nations
360 Lexington Avenue, 11th
Floor, New York, NY 10017
Tel: (212) 972 1212/1213 •
Fax: (212) 972 1216

Albania
Permanent Representative of the
Republic of Albania to the United
Nations
320 East 79th Street, New York,
NY 10021
Tel: (212) 249 2059/5654/5631 •
Fax: (212) 535 2917

Algeria
Permanent Representative of
Algeria to the United Nations
326 East 48th Street, New York,
NY 10017
Tel: (212) 750 1960/1961/1962 •
Fax: (212) 759 9538

Andorra
Permanent Representative of the
Principality of Andorra to the
United Nations
2 United Nations Plaza, 25th
Floor, New York, NY 10017
Tel: (212) 750 8064/8065 •
Fax: (212) 750 6630

Angola

Permanent Representative of the
Republic of Angola to the United
Nations
125 East 73rd Street, New York,
NY 10021
Tel: (212) 861 5656 •
Fax: (212) 861 9295

Antigua and Barbuda

Permanent Representative of
Antigua and Barbuda to the
United Nations
610 Fifth Avenue, Suite 311, New
York, NY 10020
Tel: (212) 541 4117 •
Fax: (212) 757 1607

Argentina

Permanent Representative of
Argentina to the United Nations
1 United Nations Plaza, 25th
Floor, New York, NY 10017
Tel: (212) 688 6300 •
Fax: (212) 980 8395

Armenia

Permanent Representative of the
Republic of Armenia to the
United Nations
119 East 36th Street, New York,
NY 10016
Tel: (212) 686 9079 •
Fax: (212) 686 3934

Australia

Permanent Representative of
Australia to the United Nations
150 East 42nd Street, 33rd Floor,
New York, NY 10017–5612
Tel: (212) 351 6600 •
Fax: (212) 351 6610

Austria

Permanent Representative of
Austria to the United Nations
823 United Nations Plaza, 8th
Floor, New York, NY 10017
Tel: (212) 949 1840 •
Fax: (212) 953 1302

Azerbaijan

Permanent Representative of the
Republic of Azerbaijan to the
United Nations
866 United Nations Plaza, Suite
560, New York, NY 10017
Tel: (212) 371 2559/2832/2721 •
Fax: (212) 371 2784/2672

Bahamas

Permanent Representative of the
Commonwealth of the Bahamas
to the United Nations
231 East 46th Street, New York,
NY 10017
Tel: (212) 421 6925/6926/6929 •
Fax: (212) 759 2135

Bahrain

Permanent Representative of the
State of Bahrain to the United
Nations
866 Second Avenue, 14th and
15th Floors, New York, NY 10017
Tel: (212) 223 6200 •
Fax: (212) 319 0687

Bangladesh

Permanent Representative of the
People's Republic of Bangladesh
to the United Nations
821 United Nations Plaza, 8th
Floor, New York, NY 10017
Tel: (212) 867

3434/3435/3436/3427 *or* 972
1267/1317/4310 •
Fax: (212) 972 4038

Barbados
Permanent Representative of
Barbados to the United Nations
800 Second Avenue, 2nd Floor,
New York, NY 10017
Tel: (212) 867
8431/8432/8433/8434/8435 •
Fax: (212) 986 1030

Belarus
Permanent Representative of the
Republic of Belarus to the United
Nations
136 East 67th Street, New York,
NY 10021
Tel: (212) 535 3420 •
Fax: (212) 734 4810

Belgium
Permanent Representative of
Belgium to the United Nations
823 United Nations Plaza, 4th
Floor, New York, NY 10017
Tel: (212) 378 6300 •
Fax: (212) 681 7618/7619

Belize
Permanent Representative of
Belize to the United Nations
800 Second Avenue, Suite 400G,
New York, NY 10017
Tel: (212) 599 0233 •
Fax: (212) 599 3391

Benin
Permanent Representative of the
Republic of Benin to the United
Nations

4 East 73rd Street, New York, NY
10021
Tel: (212) 249 6014, 6025 •
Fax: (212) 734 4735

Bhutan
Permanent Representative of the
Kingdom of Bhutan to the
United Nations
2 United Nations Plaza, 27th
Floor, New York, NY 10017
Tel: (212) 826 1919 •
Fax: (212) 826 2998

Bolivia
Permanent Representative of
Bolivia to the United Nations
211 East 43rd Street, 8th Floor
(Room 802), New York, NY 10017
Tel: (212) 682 8132 •
Fax: (212) 687 4642

Bosnia and Herzegovina
Permanent Representative of the
Republic of Bosnia and
Herzegovina to the United
Nations
866 United Nations Plaza, Suite
580, New York, NY 10017
Tel: (212) 751 9015 •
Fax: (212) 751 9019

Botswana
Permanent Representative of
Botswana to the United Nations
103 East 37th Street, New York,
NY 10016
Tel: (212) 889 2277/2331/2491 •
Fax: (212) 725 5061

Brazil

Permanent Representative of
Brazil to the United Nations
747 Third Avenue, 9th Floor,
New York, NY 10017
Tel: (212) 372 2600 •
Fax: (212) 371 5716

Brunei Darussalam

Permanent Representative of
Brunei Darussalam to the United
Nations
771 First Avenue, New York, NY
10017
Tel: (212) 697 3465 •
Fax: (212) 697 9889

Bulgaria

Permanent Representative of the
Republic of Bulgaria to the
United Nations
11 East 84th Street, New York,
NY 10028
Tel: (212) 737 4790/4791 *or*
327 4180/4181 •
Fax: (212) 472 9865

Burkina Faso

Permanent Representative of
Burkina Faso to the United
Nations
115 East 73rd Street, New York,
NY 10021
Tel: (212) 288 7515/7527 •
Fax: (212) 772 3562

Burundi

Permanent Representative of the
Republic of Burundi to the
United Nations
336 East 45th Street, 12th Floor,
New York, NY 10017

Tel: (212) 499
0001/0002/0003/0004/0005 •
Fax: (212) 499 0006

Cambodia

Permanent Representative of the
Kingdom of Cambodia to the
United Nations
866 United Nations Plaza, Room
420, New York, NY 10017
Tel: (212) 223 0676/0435/0530 •
Fax: (212) 223 0425

Cameroon

Permanent Representative of the
Republic of Cameroon to the
United Nations
22 East 73rd Street, New York,
NY 10021
Tel: (212) 794
2295/2296/2297/2298/2299 •
Fax: (212) 249 0533

Canada

Permanent Representative of
Canada to the United Nations
1 Dag Hammarskjöld Plaza, 885
Second Avenue, 14th Floor, New
York, NY 10017
Tel: (212) 848 1100 •
Fax: (212) 848 1192

Cape Verde

Permanent Representative of the
Republic of Cape Verde to the
United Nations
27 East 69th Street, New York,
NY 10021
Tel: (212) 472 0333 •
Fax: (212) 794 1398

Central African Republic
Permanent Representative of the
Central African Republic to the
United Nations
386 Park Avenue South, Room
1114, New York, NY 10016
Tel: (212) 679 8089/7439 •
Fax: (212) 545 8326

Chad
Permanent Representative of the
Republic of Chad to the United
Nations
211 East 43rd Street, Suite 1703,
New York, NY 10017
Tel: (212) 986 0980 •
Fax: (212) 986 0152

Chile
Permanent Representative of
Chile to the United Nations
3 Dag Hammarskjöld Plaza, 305
East 47th Street, 10th/11th Floor,
New York, NY 10017
Tel: (212) 832 3323 •
Fax: (212) 832 8714

China
Permanent Representative of the
People's Republic of China to the
United Nations
350 East 35th Street, New York,
NY 10016
Tel: (212) 655 6100 •
Fax: (212) 634 7626
Email:
chinamission_un@fmprc.gov.cn

Colombia
Permanent Representative of
Colombia to the United Nations
140 East 57th Street, 5th Floor,

New York, NY 10022
Tel: (212) 355 7776 •
Fax: (212) 371 2813

Comoros
Permanent Representative of the
Islamic Federal Republic of the
Comoros to the United Nations
420 East 50th Street, New York,
NY 10022
Tel: (212) 972 8010/8042 •
Fax: (212) 983 4712

Congo
Permanent Representative of the
Republic of the Congo to the
United Nations
14 East 65th Street, New York,
NY 10021
Tel: (212) 744 7840/7841/7842 •
Fax: (212) 744 7975

Costa Rica
Permanent Representative of
Costa Rica to the United Nations
211 East 43rd Street, Room 903,
New York, NY 10017
Tel: (212) 986 6373 •
Fax: (212) 986 6842

Côte d'Ivoire
Permanent Representative of
Côte d'Ivoire to the United
Nations
46 East 74th Street, New York,
NY 10021
Tel: (212) 717 5555 •
Fax: (212) 717 4492

Croatia
Permanent Representative of the
Republic of Croatia to the United

Nations
820 Second Avenue, 19th Floor,
New York, NY 10017
Tel: (212) 986 1585 •
Fax: (212) 986 2011

Cuba
Permanent Representative of
Cuba to the United Nations
315 Lexington Avenue and 38th
Street, New York, NY 10016
Tel: (212) 689 7215/7216/7217 •
Fax: (212) 779 1697

Cyprus
Permanent Representative of
Cyprus to the United Nations
13 East 40th Street, New York,
NY 10016
Tel: (212) 481 6023/6024/6025 •
Fax: (212) 685 7316 *or* 779 0244
or 689 5716

Czech Republic
Permanent Representative of the
Czech Republic to the United
Nations
1109 Madison Avenue, New York,
NY 10028
Tel: (212) 535 8814/8815/8818 •
Fax: (212) 772 0586

Democratic People's Republic of Korea
Permanent Representative of the
Democratic People's Republic of
Korea to the United Nations
820 Second Avenue, 13th Floor,
New York, NY 10017
Tel: (212) 972 3105/3106/3128 •
Fax: (212) 972 3154

Democratic Republic of the Congo
Permanent Representative of the
Democratic Republic of the
Congo to the United Nations
866 United Nations Plaza, Suite
511, New York, NY 10017
Tel: (212) 319 8061 •
Fax: (212) 319 8232

Denmark
Permanent Representative of
Denmark to the United Nations
1 Dag Hammarskjöld Plaza, 885
Second Avenue, 18th Floor, New
York, NY 10017–2201
Tel: (212) 308 7009/2177 •
Fax: (212) 308 3384

Djibouti
Permanent Representative of the
Republic of Djibouti to the
United Nations
866 United Nations Plaza, Suite
4011, New York, NY 10017
Tel: (212) 753 3163 •
Fax: (212) 223 1276

Dominica
Permanent Representative of the
Commonwealth of Dominica to
the United Nations
800 Second Avenue, Suite 400H,
New York, NY 10017
Tel: (212) 949 0853 •
Fax: (212) 808 4975

Dominican Republic
Permanent Representative of the
Dominican Republic to the
United Nations
144 East 44th Street, 4th Floor,

New York, NY 10017
Tel: (212) 867 0833 •
Fax: (212) 986 4694

Ecuador
Permanent Representative of
Ecuador to the United Nations
866 United Nations Plaza, Room
516, New York, NY 10017
Tel: (212) 935 1680/1681 •
Fax: (212) 935 1835

Egypt
Permanent Representative of the
Arab Republic of Egypt to the
United Nations
304 East 44th Street, New York,
NY 10017
Tel: (212) 503 0300 •
Fax: (212) 949 5999

El Salvador
Permanent Representative of El
Salvador to the United Nations
46 Park Avenue, New York, NY
10016
Tel: (212) 679 1616/1617 •
Fax: (212) 725 7831

Equatorial Guinea
Permanent Representative of
Equatorial Guinea to the United
Nations
57 Magnolia Avenue, Mount
Vernon, NY 10553
Tel: (914) 667 8999 •
Fax: (914) 667 8778

Eritrea
Permanent Representative of
Eritrea to the United Nations
800 Second Avenue, 18th Floor,

New York, NY 10017
Tel: (212) 687 3390 •
Fax: (212) 687 3138

Estonia
Permanent Representative of the
Republic of Estonia to the United
Nations
600 Third Avenue, 26th Floor,
New York, NY 10016–2001
Tel: (212) 883 0640 •
Fax: (212) 883 0648

Ethiopia
Permanent Representative of the
Federal Democratic Republic of
Ethiopia to the United Nations
866 Second Avenue, 3rd Floor,
New York, NY 10017
Tel: (212) 421 1830 •
Fax: (212) 754 0360

Fiji
Permanent Representative of the
Republic of the Fiji Islands to the
United Nations
630 Third Avenue, 7th Floor,
New York, NY 10017
Tel: (212) 687 4130 •
Fax: (212) 687 3963

Finland
Permanent Representative of
Finland to the United Nations
866 United Nations Plaza, Suite
222, New York, NY 10017
Tel: (212) 355 2100 •
Fax: (212) 759 6156

Former Yugoslav Republic of Macedonia
Permanent Representative of the

Former Yugoslav Republic of Macedonia to the United Nations
866 United Nations Plaza, Suite 517, New York, NY 10017
Tel: (212) 308 8504/8723 •
Fax: (212) 308 8724

France
Permanent Representative of France to the United Nations
1 Dag Hammarskjöld Plaza, 245 East 47th Street, 44th Floor, New York, NY 10017
Tel: (212) 308 5700 •
Fax: (212) 421 6889

Gabon
Permanent Representative of the Gabonese Republic to the United Nations
18 East 41st Street, 9th Floor, New York, NY 10017
Tel: (212) 686 9720 •
Fax: (212) 689 5769

Gambia
Permanent Representative of the Gambia to the United Nations
800 Second Avenue, Suite 400F, New York, NY 10017
Tel: (212) 949 6640 •
Fax: (212) 808 4975

Georgia
Permanent Representative of Georgia to the United Nations
1 United Nations Plaza, 26th Floor, New York, NY 10017
Tel: (212) 759 1949 •
Fax: (212) 759 1832

Germany
Permanent Representative of Germany to the United Nations
871 United Nations Plaza (First Avenue and 48th/49th Streets), New York, NY 10017–1814
Tel: (212) 940 0400 •
Fax: (212) 940 0402

Ghana
Permanent Representative of Ghana to the United Nations
19 East 47th Street, New York, NY 10017
Tel: (212) 832 1300 •
Fax: (212) 751 6743

Greece
Permanent Representative of Greece to the United Nations
866 Second Avenue, 13th Floor, New York, NY 10017–2905
Tel: (212) 888 6900 •
Fax: (212) 888 4440

Grenada
Permanent Representative of Grenada to the United Nations
800 Second Avenue, Suite 400K, New York, NY 10017
Tel: (212) 599 0301/0302 •
Fax: (212) 599 1540

Guatemala
Permanent Representative of Guatemala to the United Nations
57 Park Avenue, New York, NY 10016
Tel: (212) 679 4760 •
Fax: (212) 685 8741

Guinea
Permanent Representative of the
Republic of Guinea to the United
Nations
140 East 39th Street, New York,
NY 10016
Tel: (212) 687 8115/8116/8117 •
Fax: (212) 687 8248

Guinea-Bissau
Permanent Representative of the
Republic of Guinea-Bissau to the
United Nations
211 East 43rd Street, Room 704,
New York, NY 10017
Tel: (212) 338 9394/9380 •
Fax: (212) 293 0264

Guyana
Permanent Representative of the
Republic of Guyana to the
United Nations
866 United Nations Plaza, Suite
555, New York, NY 10017
Tel: (212) 527 3232/3233 •
Fax: (212) 935 7548

Haiti
Permanent Representative of
Haiti to the United Nations
801 Second Avenue, Room 600,
New York, NY 10017
Tel: (212) 370 4840 •
Fax: (212) 661 8698

Honduras
Permanent Representative of
Honduras to the United Nations
866 United Nations Plaza, Suite
417, New York, NY 10017
Tel: (212) 752 3370/3371 •
Fax: (212) 223 0498 *or* 751 0403

Hungary
Permanent Representative of the
Republic of Hungary to the
United Nations
227 East 52nd Street, New York,
NY 10022
Tel: (212) 752 0209 *or* 755
5419/4594/6290 •
Fax: (212) 755 5395

Iceland
Permanent Representative of
Iceland to the United Nations
800 Third Avenue, 36th Floor,
New York, NY 10022
Tel: (212) 593 2700 •
Fax: (212) 593 6269

India
Permanent Representative of
India to the United Nations
235 East 43rd Street, New York,
NY 10017
Tel: (212) 490 9660 •
Fax: (212) 490 9656

Indonesia
Permanent Representative of the
Republic of Indonesia to the
United Nations
325 East 38th Street, New York,
NY 10016
Tel: (212) 972 8333 •
Fax: (212) 972 9780

Iran (Islamic Republic of)
Permanent Representative of the
Islamic Republic of Iran to the
United Nations
622 Third Avenue, 34th Floor,
New York, NY 10017
Tel: (212) 687 2020 •
Fax: (212) 867 7086

Iraq
Permanent Representative of
Iraq to the United Nations
14 East 79th Street, New York,
NY 10021
Tel: (212) 737 4433 •
Fax: (212) 772 1794

Ireland
Permanent Representative of
Ireland to the United Nations
1 Dag Hammarskjöld Plaza, 885
Second Avenue, 19th Floor, New
York, NY 10017
Tel: (212) 421 6934 •
Fax: (212) 752 4726

Israel
Permanent Representative of
Israel to the United Nations
800 Second Avenue, New York,
NY 10017
Tel: (212) 499 5510 •
Fax: (212) 499 5515

Italy
Permanent Representative of
Italy to the United Nations
2 United Nations Plaza, 24th
Floor, New York, NY 10017
Tel: (212) 486 9191 •
Fax: (212) 486 1036

Jamaica
Permanent Representative of
Jamaica to the United Nations
767 Third Avenue, 9th Floor,
New York, NY 10017
Tel: (212) 935 7509 •
Fax: (212) 935 7607

Japan
Permanent Representative of
Japan to the United Nations
866 United Nations Plaza, 2nd
Floor, New York, NY 10017
Tel: (212) 223 4300 •
Fax: (212) 751 1966

Jordan
Permanent Representative of the
Hashemite Kingdom of Jordan to
the United Nations
866 United Nations Plaza, Suite
552, New York, NY 10017
Tel: (212) 752 0135, 0136 •
Fax: (212) 826 0830

Kazakhstan
Permanent Representative of the
Republic of Kazakhstan to the
United Nations
866 United Nations Plaza, Suite
586, New York, NY 10017
Tel: (212) 230 1900/1192 •
Fax: (212) 230 1172

Kenya
Permanent Representative of the
Republic of Kenya to the United
Nations
866 United Nations Plaza, Room
486, New York, NY 10017
Tel: (212) 421 4740 •
Fax: (212) 486 1985

Kiribati
At the time of publication,
Kiribati does not have
representation in New York.

Kuwait
Permanent Representative of the
State of Kuwait to the United
Nations
321 East 44th Street, New York,
NY 10017
Tel: (212) 973 4300 •
Fax: (212) 370 1733

Kyrgyzstan
Permanent Representative of the
Kyrgyz Republic to the United
Nations
866 United Nations Plaza, Suite
477, New York, NY 10017
Tel: (212) 486 4214/4654 •
Fax: (212) 486 5259

**Lao People's Democratic
Republic**
Permanent Representative of the
Lao People's Democratic
Republic to the United Nations
317 East 51st Street, New York,
NY 10022
Tel: (212) 832 2734/0095 •
Fax: (212) 750 0039

Latvia
Permanent Representative of the
Republic of Latvia to the United
Nations
333 East 50th Street, New York,
NY 10022
Tel: (212) 838 8877 •
Fax: (212) 838 8920

Lebanon
Permanent Representative of
Lebanon to the United Nations
866 United Nations Plaza, Room
531–533, New York, NY 10017

Tel: (212) 355 5460/5461 •
Fax: (212) 838 2819

Lesotho
Permanent Representative of the
Kingdom of Lesotho to the
United Nations
204 East 39th Street, New York,
NY 10016
Tel: (212) 661
1690/1691/1692/1693 •
Fax: (212)682 4388

Liberia
Permanent Representative of the
Republic of Liberia to the United
Nations
820 Second Avenue, 13th Floor,
New York, NY 10017
Tel: (212) 687 1033/1034 •
Fax: (212) 687 1035, 1846

Libyan Arab Jamahiriya
Permanent Representative of the
Socialist People's Libyan Arab
Jamahiriya to the United Nations
309–315 East 48th Street, New
York, NY 10017
Tel: (212) 752 5775 •
Fax: (212) 593 4787

Liechtenstein
Permanent Representative of the
Principality of Liechtenstein to
the United Nations
633 Third Avenue, 27th Floor,
New York, NY 10017
Tel: (212) 599 0220 •
Fax: (212) 599 0064

Lithuania
Permanent Representative of the Republic of Lithuania to the United Nations
420 Fifth Avenue, 3rd Floor, New York, NY 10018
Tel: (212) 354 7820 •
Fax: (212) 354 7833

Luxembourg
Permanent Representative of Luxembourg to the United Nations
17 Beekman Place, New York, NY 10022
Tel: (212) 935 3589 •
Fax: (212) 935 5896

Madagascar
Permanent Representative of the Republic of Madagascar to the United Nations
820 Second Avenue, Suite 800, New York, NY 10017
Tel: (212) 986 9491/9492 •
Fax: (212) 986 6271

Malawi
Permanent Representative of the Republic of Malawi to the United Nations
600 Third Avenue, 21st Floor, New York, NY 10016
Tel: (212) 949 0180/0181/0182 •
Fax: (212) 599 5021

Malaysia
Permanent Representative of Malaysia to the United Nations
313 East 43rd Street, New York, NY 10017
Tel: (212) 986 6310 •
Fax: (212) 490 8576

Maldives
Permanent Representative of the Republic of Maldives to the United Nations
800 Second Avenue, Suite 400E, New York, NY 10017
Tel: (212) 599 6194/6195 •
Fax: (212) 661 6405

Mali
Permanent Representative of the Republic of Mali to the United Nations
111 East 69th Street, New York, NY 10021
Tel: (212) 737 4150 or 794 1311 •
Fax: (212) 472 3778

Malta
Permanent Representative of Malta to the United Nations
249 East 35th Street, New York, NY 10016
Tel: (212) 725 2345 •
Fax: (212) 779 7097

Marshall Islands
Permanent Representative of the Republic of the Marshall Islands to the United Nations
800 Second Avenue, 18th Floor, New York, NY 10017
Tel: (212) 983 3040 •
Fax: (212) 983 3202

Mauritania
Permanent Representative of the Islamic Republic of Mauritania to the United Nations
211 East 43rd Street, Suite 2000, New York, NY 10017
Tel: (212) 986 7963/8189 •
Fax: (212) 986 8419

Mauritius

Permanent Representative of the
Republic of Mauritius to the
United Nations
211 East 43rd Street, 15th Floor,
New York, NY 10017
Tel: (212) 949 0190/0191 •
Fax: (212) 697 3829

Mexico

Permanent Representative of
Mexico to the United Nations
2 United Nations Plaza, 28th
Floor, New York, NY 10017
Tel: (212) 752 0220 •
Fax: (212) 688 8862

Micronesia (Federated States of)

Permanent Representative of the
Federated States of Micronesia
to the United Nations
820 Second Avenue, Suite 17A,
New York, NY 10017
Tel: (212) 697 8370 •
Fax: (212) 697 8295

Monaco

Permanent Representative of the
Principality of Monaco to the
United Nations
866 United Nations Plaza, Suite
520, New York, NY 10017
Tel: (212) 832 0721 •
Fax: (212) 832 5358

Mongolia

Permanent Representative of
Mongolia to the United Nations
6 East 77th Street, New York, NY
10021
Tel: (212) 861 9460/472 6517 •
Fax: (212) 861 9464

Morocco

Permanent Representative of the
Kingdom of Morocco to the
United Nations
866 Second Avenue, 6th and 7th
Floors, New York, NY 10017
Tel: (212) 421 1580 •
Fax: (212) 980 1512

Mozambique

Permanent Representative of the
Republic of Mozambique to the
United Nations
420 East 50th Street, New York,
NY 10022
Tel: (212) 644 5965 •
Fax: (212) 644 5972

Myanmar

Permanent Representative of the
Union of Myanmar to the United
Nations
10 East 77th Street, New York,
NY 10021
Tel: (212) 535 1310/1311 •
Fax: (212) 737 2421

Namibia

Permanent Representative of the
Republic of Namibia to the
United Nations
135 East 36th Street, New York,
NY 10016
Tel: (212) 685 2003 •
Fax: (212) 685 1561

Nauru

Permanent Representative of the
Republic of Nauru to the United
Nations
800 Second Avenue, Suite 400D,
New York, NY 10017
Tel: (212) 937 0074 •
Fax: (212) 937 0079

Nepal

Permanent Representative of the Kingdom of Nepal to the United Nations
820 Second Avenue, Suite 17B, New York, NY 10017
Tel: (212) 370 3988/3989 •
Fax: (212) 953 2038

The Netherlands

Permanent Representative of the Kingdom of The Netherlands to the United Nations
235 East 45th Street, 16th Floor, New York, NY 10017
Tel: (212) 697 5547 •
Fax: (212) 370 1954

New Zealand

Permanent Representative of New Zealand to the United Nations
1 United Nations Plaza, 25th Floor, New York, NY 10017
Tel: (212) 826 1960 •
Fax: (212) 758 0827

Nicaragua

Permanent Representative of Nicaragua to the United Nations
820 Second Avenue, 8th Floor, New York, NY 10017
Tel: (212) 490 7997 •
Fax: (212) 286 0815

Niger

Permanent Representative of the Niger to the United Nations
417 East 50th Street, New York, NY 10022
Tel: (212) 421 3260/3261/3286 •
Fax: (212) 753 6931

Nigeria

Permanent Representative of Nigeria to the United Nations
828 Second Avenue, New York, NY 10017
Tel: (212) 953 9130 •
Fax: (212) 697 1970

Norway

Permanent Representative of Norway to the United Nations
825 Third Avenue, 39th Floor, New York, NY 10022
Tel: (212) 421 0280/0281/0282/0283/0284 •
Fax: (212) 688 0554

Oman

Permanent Representative of the Sultanate of Oman to the United Nations
866 United Nations Plaza, Suite 540, New York, NY 10017
Tel: (212) 355 3505/3506/3507 •
Fax: (212) 644 0070

Pakistan

Permanent Representative of Pakistan to the United Nations
Pakistan House, 8 East 65th Street, New York, NY 10021
Tel: (212) 879 8600 •
Fax: (212) 744 7348

Palau

At the time of publication, Palau does not have representation in New York.

Panama

Permanent Representative of Panama to the United Nations
866 United Nations Plaza, Suite

4030, New York, NY 10017
Tel: (212) 421 5420/5421 •
Fax: (212) 421 2694

Papua New Guinea
Permanent Representative of
Papua New Guinea to the United
Nations
201 East 42nd Street, Suite 405,
New York, NY 10017
Tel: (212) 557 5001 •
Fax: (212) 557 5009

Paraguay
Permanent Representative of
Paraguay to the United Nations
211 East 43rd Street, Suite 400,
New York, NY 10017
Tel: (212) 687 3490/3491 •
Fax: (212) 818 1282

Peru
Permanent Representative of
Peru to the United Nations
820 Second Avenue, Suite 1600,
New York, NY 10017
Tel: (212) 687 3336 •
Fax: (212) 972 6975

Philippines
Permanent Representative of the
Republic of the Philippines to
the United Nations
556 Fifth Avenue, 5th floor, New
York, NY 10036
Tel: (212) 764
1300/1301/1302/1303/1304 *or*
704 7322 •
Fax: (212) 840 8602

Poland
Permanent Representative of the
Republic of Poland to the United
Nations
9 East 66th Street, New York, NY
10021
Tel: (212) 744 2506 •
Fax: (212) 517 6771

Portugal
Permanent Representative of
Portugal to the United Nations
866 Second Avenue, 9th Floor,
New York, NY 10017
Tel: (212) 759
9444/9445/9446/9447 •
Fax: (212) 355 1124

Qatar
Permanent Representative of the
State of Qatar to the United
Nations
809 United Nations Plaza, 4th
Floor, New York, NY 10017
Tel: (212) 486 9335/9336 •
Fax: (212) 758 4952 *or* 308 5630

Republic of Korea
Permanent Representative of the
Republic of Korea to the United
Nations
335 East 45th Street, New York,
NY 10017
Tel: (212) 439 4000 •
Fax: (212) 986 1083

Republic of Moldova
Permanent Representative of the
Republic of Moldova to the
United Nations
573–577 Third Avenue, New
York, NY 10016
Tel: (212) 682 3523 •
Fax: (212) 682 6274

Romania
Permanent Representative of Romania to the United Nations
573–577 Third Avenue, New York, NY 10016
Tel: (212) 682 3273/3274 *or* 818 1491/1496 •
Fax: (212) 682 9746

Russian Federation
Permanent Representative of the Russian Federation to the United Nations
136 East 67th Street, New York, NY 10021
Tel: (212) 861 4900/4901/4902 •
Fax: (212) 628 0252

Rwanda
Permanent Representative of the Rwandese Republic to the United Nations
124 East 39th Street, New York, NY 10016
Tel: (212) 679 9010/9023/9024 •
Fax: (212) 679 9133

Saint Kitts and Nevis
Permanent Representative of Saint Kitts and Nevis to the United Nations
414 East 75th Street, 5th Floor, New York, NY 10021
Tel: (212) 535 1234 •
Fax: (212) 535 6854

Saint Lucia
Permanent Representative of Saint Lucia to the United Nations
800 Second Avenue, 9th Floor, New York, NY 10017
Tel: (212) 697 9360/9361 •
Fax: (212) 697 4993

Saint Vincent and the Grenadines
Permanent Representative of Saint Vincent and the Grenadines to the United Nations
801 Second Avenue, 21st Floor, New York, NY 10017
Tel: (212) 599 0950 •
Fax: (212) 599 1020

Samoa
Permanent Representative of the Independent State of Samoa to the United Nations
800 Second Avenue, Suite 400J, New York, NY 10017
Tel: (212) 599 6196/6197 •
Fax: (212) 599 0797 *or* 972 3970

San Marino
Permanent Representative of the Republic of San Marino to the United Nations
327 East 50th Street, New York, NY 10022
Tel: (212) 751 1234 •
Fax: (212) 751 1436

Sao Tome and Principe
Permanent Representative of Sao Tome and Principe to the United Nations
400 Park Avenue, 7th Floor, New York, NY 10022
Tel: (212) 317 0533 •
Fax: (212) 317 0580

Saudi Arabia
Permanent Representative of
Saudi Arabia to the United
Nations
405 Lexington Avenue, 56th
Floor, New York, NY 10017
Tel: (212) 697 4830 •
Fax: (212) 983 4895

Senegal
Permanent Representative of the
Republic of Senegal to the
United Nations
238 East 68th Street, New York,
NY 10021
Tel: (212) 517 9030/9031/9032 •
Fax: (212) 517 7628

Seychelles
Permanent Representative of the
Republic of Seychelles to the
United Nations
800 Second Avenue, Suite 400C,
New York, NY 10017
Tel: (212) 972 1785 •
Fax: (212) 972 1786

Sierra Leone
Permanent Representative of the
Republic of Sierra Leone to the
United Nations
245 East 49th Street, New York,
NY 10017
Tel: (212) 688 1656/4985 •
Fax: (212) 688 4924

Singapore
Permanent Representative of the
Republic of Singapore to the
United Nations
231 East 51st Street, New York,
NY 10022

Tel: (212) 826
0840/0841/0842/0843/0844 •
Fax: (212) 826 2964

Slovakia
Permanent Representative of the
Slovak Republic to the United
Nations
866 United Nations Plaza, Suite
494, New York, NY 10017
Tel: (212) 980 1558/3308/3235 •
Fax: (212) 980 3295

Slovenia
Permanent Representative of
Slovenia to the United Nations
600 Third Avenue, 24th Floor,
New York, NY 10016
Tel: (212) 370 3007/1831 •
Fax: (212) 370 1824

Solomon Islands
Permanent Representative of
Solomon Islands to the United
Nations
800 Second Avenue, Suite 400L,
New York, NY 10017
Tel: (212) 599 6192/6193 •
Fax: (212) 661 8925

Somalia
Permanent Representative of the
Somali Republic to the United
Nations
425 East 61st Street, Suite 702,
New York, NY 10021
Tel: (212) 688 9410 •
Fax: (212) 7590651

South Africa
Permanent Representative of the
Republic of South Africa to the

United Nations
333 East 38th Street, 9th Floor,
New York, NY 10016
Tel: (212) 213 5583 •
Fax: (212) 692 2498

Spain

Permanent Representative of
Spain to the United Nations
823 United Nations Plaza, 345
East 46th Street, 9th Floor, New
York, NY 10017
Tel: (212) 661 1050 •
Fax: (212) 949 7247

Sri Lanka

Permanent Representative of the
Democratic Socialist Republic of
Sri Lanka to the United Nations
630 Third Avenue, 20th Floor,
New York, NY 10017
Tel: (212) 986 7040/7043 •
Fax: (212) 986 1838

Sudan

Permanent Representative of the
Republic of the Sudan to the
United Nations
655 Third Avenue, Suite
500–510, New York, NY 10017
Tel: (212) 573
6033/6035/6038/6039 •
Fax: (212) 573 6160

Suriname

Permanent Representative of the
Republic of Suriname to the
United Nations
866 United Nations Plaza, Suite
320, New York, NY 10017
Tel: (212) 826 0660 •
Fax: (212) 980 7029

Swaziland

Permanent Representative of the
Kingdom of Swaziland to the
United Nations
408 East 50th Street, New York,
NY 10022
Tel: (212) 371 8910 •
Fax: (212) 754 2755

Sweden

Permanent Representative of
Sweden to the United Nations
1 Dag Hammarskjöld Plaza, 885
Second Avenue, 46th Floor, New
York, NY 10017–2201
Tel: (212) 583 2500 •
Fax: (212) 832 0389

Switzerland

Permanent Representative of
Switzerland to the United
Nations
633 Third Avenue, 29th Floor,
New York, NY 10017
Tel: (212) (212) 286 1540 •
Fax: (212) 286 1555

Syrian Arab Republic

Permanent Representative of the
Syrian Arab Republic to the
United Nations
820 Second Avenue, 15th Floor,
New York, NY 10017
Tel: (212) 661 1313 •
Fax: (212) 983 4439

Tajikistan

Permanent Representative of the
Republic of Tajikistan to the
United Nations
136 East 67th Street, New York,
NY 10021

Tel: (212) 744 2196 •
Fax: (212) 472 7645

Thailand
Permanent Representative of
Thailand to the United Nations
351 East 52nd Street, New York,
NY 10022
Tel: (212) 754 2230/2231 •
Fax: (212) 754 2535 *or* 688 3029

Togo
Permanent Representative of
Togo to the United Nations
112 East 40th Street, New York,
NY 10016
Tel: (212) 490 3455/3456 •
Fax: (212) 983 6684

Tonga
Permanent Representative of the
Kingdom of Tonga to the United
Nations
250 East 51st Street, New York,
NY 10022
Tel: (917) 369 1025 •
Fax: (917) 369 1024

Trinidad and Tobago
Permanent Representative of the
Republic of Trinidad and Tobago
to the United Nations
820 Second Avenue, 5th Floor,
New York, NY 10017
Tel: (212) 697
7620/7621/7622/7623 •
Fax: (212) 682 3580

Tunisia
Permanent Representative of
Tunisia to the United Nations
31 Beekman Place, New York,

NY 10022
Tel: (212) 751 7503/7534/5069 •
Fax: (212) 751 0569

Turkey
Permanent Representative of
Turkey to the United Nations
821 United Nations Plaza, 10th
Floor, New York, NY 10017
Tel: (212) 949 0150 •
Fax: (212) 949 0086

Turkmenistan
Permanent Representative of
Turkmenistan to the United
Nations
866 United Nations Plaza, Suite
424, New York, NY 10017
Tel: (212) 486 8908 •
Fax: (212) 486 2521

Tuvalu
Permanent Representative of
Tuvalu to the United Nations
800 Second Avenue, Suite 400B,
New York, NY 10017
Tel: (212) 490 0534 •
Fax: (212) 808 4975

Uganda
Permanent Representative of the
Republic of Uganda to the
United Nations
336 East 45th Street, New York,
NY 10017
Tel: (212) 949 0110/0113 •
Fax: (212) 687 4517

Ukraine
Permanent Representative of
Ukraine to the United Nations
220 East 51st Street, New York,

NY 10022
Tel: (212) 759 7003 •
Fax: (212) 355 9455

United Arab Emirates
Permanent Representative of the
United Arab Emirates to the
United Nations
747 Third Avenue, 36th Floor,
New York, NY 10017
Tel: (212) 371 0480 •
Fax: (212) 371 4923

**United Kingdom of Great
Britain and Northern Ireland**
Permanent Representative of the
United Kingdom to the United
Nations
1 Dag Hammarskjöld Plaza, 885
Second Avenue, New York, NY
10017
Tel: (212) 745 9200 •
Fax: (212) 745 9316

United Republic of Tanzania
Permanent Representative of the
United Republic of Tanzania to
the United Nations
205 East 42nd Street, 13th Floor,
New York, NY 10017
Tel: (212) 972 9160 •
Fax: (212) 682 5232

United States of America
Permanent Representative of the
United States to the United
Nations
799 United Nations Plaza, New
York, NY 10017–3505
Tel: (212) 415 4000 •
Fax: (212) 415 4443

Uruguay
Permanent Representative of
Uruguay to the United Nations
866 United Nations Plaza, Suite
322, New York, NY 10017
Tel: (212) 752 8240/8241 •
Fax: (212) 593 0935

Uzbekistan
Permanent Representative of the
Republic of Uzbekistan to the
United Nations
866 United Nations Plaza, Suite
326, New York, NY 10017–7671
Tel: (212) 486 4242 •
Fax: (212) 486 7998

Vanuatu
Permanent Representative of the
Republic of Vanuatu to the
United Nations
42 Broadway, Suite 1200–12–18,
New York, NY 10004
Tel: (212) 425 9600 •
Fax: (212) 425 9653

Venezuela
Permanent Representative of
Venezuela to the United Nations
335 East 46th Street, New York,
NY 10017
Tel: (212) 557 2055 •
Fax: (212) 557 3528

Viet Nam
Permanent Representative of the
Socialist Republic of Viet Nam to
the United Nations
866 United Nations Plaza, Suite
435, New York, NY 10017
Tel: (212) 644 0594 •
Fax: (212) 644 5732

Yemen
Permanent Representative of the
Republic of Yemen to the United
Nations
413 East 51st Street, New York,
NY 10022
Tel: (212) 355 1730/1731 •
Fax: (212) 750 9613

Yugoslavia
Permanent Representative of the
Federal Republic of Yugoslavia to
the United Nations
854 Fifth Avenue, New York, NY
10021
Tel: (212) 879 8700 •
Fax: (212) 879 8705

Zambia
Permanent Representative of the
Republic of Zambia to the United
Nations
800 Second Avenue, 9th Floor,
New York, NY 10017
Tel: (212) 972 7200 •
Fax: (212) 972 7360

Zimbabwe
Permanent Representative of the
Republic of Zimbabwe to the
United Nations
128 East 56th Street, New York,
NY 10022
Tel: (212) 980 9511/5084 •
Fax: (212) 308 6705

MAPS OF THE UN IN GENEVA AND NEW YORK

These maps are to help you orientate yourself to the UN buildings. It is always easier to find the coffee bar if you know where it is!

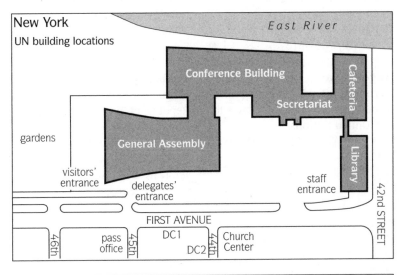

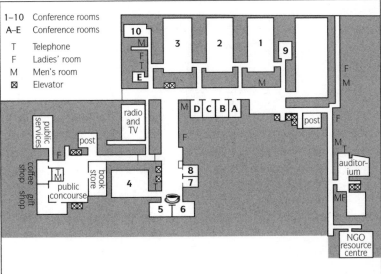

Figure 6.1 *Maps of the UN building and the conference level in New York*

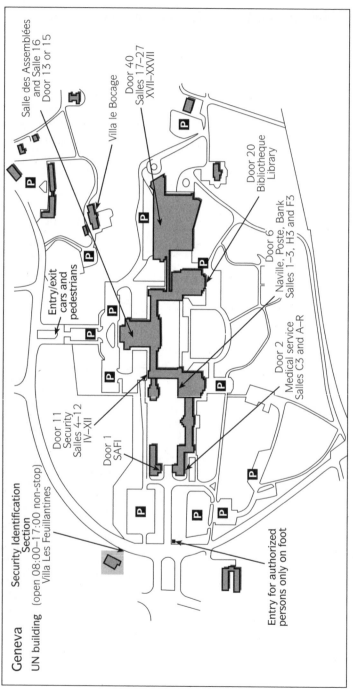

Figure 6.2 *Map of the UN building in Geneva*

UN Addresses in Geneva and New York

Geneva

CITES
Secretariat of the Convention on International Trade in Endangered Species International Environment House, Chemin des Anémones, 1219 Châtelaine, Genève
Tel: +41 22 917 8139/8140
www.cites.org

ILO
International Labour Organization
Route des Morillons 4, 1211 Genève 22
Tel: +41 22 799 6111
www.ilo.org

ITU
International Telecommunication Union
Place des Nations, 1211 Genève 20
Tel: +41 22 730 5111
www.itu.int/home

NGLS
United Nations Non-Governmental Liaison Service
Palais des Nations, 1211 Genève
Fax: +41 22 917 0432
Email: ngls@unctad.org
www.unsystem.org/ngls

SBC
Secretary of the Basel Convention
International Environmental House, Chemin des Anemones 13–15, 1219 Chatelaine, Genève
Tel: +41 22 917 8218
www.basel.int

UNAIDS
Joint United Nations Programme on HIV/AIDS
Avenue Appia 20, 1211 Genève 27
Tel: +41 22 791 3666
www.unaids.org

UNCTAD
United Nations Conference on Trade and Development
Palais des Nations, Av de la Paix 8–14, 1211 Genève 10
Tel: +41 22 907 1234
www.unctad.org

UNECE
United Nations Economic Commission for Europe
Palais des Nations, 1211 Genève 10
Tel: +41 22 917 4444
www.unece.org

UNEP
United Nations Environment Programme, European Office
International Environment House, Chemin des Anemones 11–13, 1219 Chatelaine, Genève

Tel: +41 22 917 8279
www.unep.org

UNHCR
United Nations High
Commissioner for Refugees
Avenue de la Paix 8–14, 1211
Genève 10
Tel: +41 22 917 9000
www.unhcr.ch

UNIDO
United Nations Industrial
Development Organization
Palais des Nations, Le Bocage,
Pavillion 1, 1211 Genève 10
Tel: +41 22 917 3367
www.unido.org

UNITAR
United Nations Institute for
Training and Research
International Environment
House, Chemin des Anemones
11–13, 1219 Chatelaine, Genève
Tel: +41 22 917 1234
www.unitar.org

WFP
World Food Programme
Palais des Nations, 1211 Genève
10
Tel: +41 22 917 8568
www.wfp.org

WHO
World Health Organization
Avenue Appia 20, 1211, Genève
27
Tel: +41 22 791 2111
www.who.int

WIPO
World Intellectual Property
Organization
Palais des Nations, 1211 Genève
20
Tel: +41 22 338 9111
www.wipo.int

WMO
World Meteorological
Organization
Avenue de la Paix 7 bis, 1211
Genève 2
Tel: +41 22 780 8315
www.wmo.ch

WTO
World Trade Organization
Centre William Rappard, Rue de
Lausanne 154, 1211 Genève 21
Tel: +41 22 739 5111
www.wto.org

New York

DAW
United Nations Division for the
Advancement of Women
1 United Nations Plaza, New
York, NY 10017
Tel: +1 212 963 3139
Outreach Chief: Amina Adam
www.un.org/esa

DSD
United Nations Division for
Social Development
2 United Nations Plaza, New
York, NY 10017

Focal Point for NGOs:
Mr Yao N'Goran
Tel: +1 212 963 3175

Focal Point for Major Groups:
Zehra Aydin Sipos
Tel: +1 212 963 8811
www.un.org/esa

NGLS
United Nations Non-Governmental Liaison Service
1 United Nations Plaza, DC1-1106, New York, NY 10017
Tel: +1 212 963 3125
Fax: +1 212 963 8712
ngls@un.org
www.unsystem.org/ngls
NGO unit in the Department of Economic and Social Affairs (DESA): 1 United Nations Plaza, 14th floor
(For accreditation)
Tel: + 1 212 963 8652 • Fax: + 1 212 963 9248 *or* 963 4114
Contact: Hanifa Mezoui
(mezoui@un.org)
Pass Office: North-west corner of 1st Avenue and 45th Street
(Security Pass collection)

UNCTAD
UN Conference on Trade and Development
2 United Nations Plaza, New York, NY 10017
Tel: +1 212 963 4319
www.unctad.org

UNDP
United Nations Development Programme
1 United Nations Plaza, New York, NY 10017
Tel: +1 212 906 5000
www.undp.org

UNEP
United Nations Environment Programme
2 United Nations Plaza, New York, NY 10017
Tel: +1 212 963 8144
www.unep.org

UN-Habitat
UN Human Settlements Programme
2 United Nations Plaza, New York, NY 10017
Tel: +1 212 963 5464
www.unhabitat.org

Useful Web Resources

European Union	www.europa.eu.int
Food and Agricultural Organization	www.fao.org
Global Environmental Facility	www.gefweb.org
Group of 77	www.G77.org
International Institute for Sustainable Development (IISD) Linkages (including *Earth Negotiations Bulletin*)	www.iisd.ca
International Labour Organization	www.ilo.org
International Monetary Fund	www.imf.org
International Organization of la Francophonie	www.francophonie.org
NGO–NGO Link (lists UN and related events for NGOs in NY)	www.ngos.net/events/upcoming
Non-Governmental Liaison Service	www.unsystem.org/ngls
Organisation for Economic Co-operation and Development	www.oecd.org
Organization of the Islamic Conference	www.oic-un.org
Stakeholder Forum for Our Common Future	www.stakeholderforum.org
UN Daily Journal	www.un.org/docs/journal
United Nations	www.un.org
United Nations Children's Fund	www.unicef.org
United Nations Conference on Trade and Development	www.unctad.org
United Nations Development Programme	www.undp.org
United Nations Educational, Scientific and Cultural Organization	www.unesco.org
United Nations Environment Programme	www.unep.org
United Nations Programme on HIV/AIDS	www.unaids.org
World Bank	www.worldbank.org
World Food Programme	www.wfp.org
World Health Organization	www.who.org
World Trade Organization	www.wto.org

List of Key Countries To Lobby

There are over 200 countries in the UN. If you are lobbying, it is important to start working with the ones that are most active. This list gives you 27 to start with.

Country	Name of delegate	For or against?	Mobile telephone number
Brazil (key G77 regional power)			
Canada (non-bloc country)			
China (key G77 country and UN Security Council member)			
Colombia (key regional player)			
Czech Republic (key country in transition and future EU member)			
Denmark (usually progressive EU member)			
Egypt (key G77 regional power)			
France (key EU country and UN Security Council member)			
Germany (key EU country with progressive government)			
India (key G77 regional power)			
Indonesia (key G77 regional power)			
Iran (key G77 regional power and OPEC member)			
Japan (key non-bloc developed country)			
Malaysia (key G77 regional power)			

New Zealand (key non-bloc progressive government)			
Nigeria (key G77 regional power)			
Norway (non-bloc country, usually progressive)			
Pakistan (key G77 regional power)			
Russia (key global player, non-bloc and UN Security Council member)			
Saudi Arabia (key G77 regional power and OPEC member)			
South Africa (key G77 regional power)			
Sweden (key EU member, usually progressive)			
Switzerland (non-bloc country, usually progressive)			
Uganda (progressive African country)			
United Kingdom (key EU country and UN Security Council member)			
United States (key power, non-bloc and UN Security Council member)			
Venezuela (key G77 regional power and member of OPEC)			
Other countries			

NGO Issue Caucuses and Stakeholder Groups

As mentioned before, although stakeholders will operate as individual organizations, much time is spent in trying to work together. There are some obvious benefits of this:

- coordination of information;
- agreement on positions (governments listen to coalitions as they represent a larger common view and it is easier for them to take in one or two views as opposed to hundreds);
- booking of rooms;
- sharing costs for replication of material;
- sharing costs for hardware equipment.

From 1997 to 2001, I was co-chair of the Commission on Sustainable Development (CSD) NGO Steering Committee. The committee acted as the main space for coordinating NGOs at the CSD. During that time we introduced some very useful norms and standards. I would like to take you through a few that might be useful.

The norms for a caucus were as follows:

- Issue caucuses had to be recognized by the CSD NGO Steering Committee.
- Membership in caucuses was only on an organizational basis, as opposed to individually. Any accredited NGO could become a member of any caucus.
- Issue caucuses had to consist of at least ten accredited NGOs.
- A registration of the members of each caucus was kept by the steering committee and by the caucus.
- Issue caucuses had to have one coordinator from the North and one from the South: one woman and one man.
- If a caucus was unable to hold an election due to little or no attendance at a session of the CSD, the caucus became inactive. It remained on the mailing list but had no vote on the steering committee. In the case of an inactive caucus wishing to become active (for example, in May to work on papers for the following year), a postal ballot was conducted at the time that the caucus wished to become active (for example, in May).
- Each issue caucus presented a one-paragraph statement of purpose reflecting the issues to be covered and not the positions to be taken. The statement of purpose did not allow people or organizations to be excluded from a caucus. The steering

committee could deal with any problem about membership in a caucus due to interpretation of issues.

- A person could lose membership of a caucus for a specific cause, which may have included repeated failure to follow the rules of order and procedure. In case of a charge for cause, the due process is that the matter would be referred to the process sub-committee for recommendation to the steering committee, which would make a decision. The steering committee might find that the cause of the problem was not the person who was charged.
- Where differences or disputes existed between caucuses, in the first instance the caucuses would attempt to resolve the issues by consultation. Where this failed, the matter would be taken to the management committee.

The introduction of norms was to help the smaller NGOs, particularly those from developing countries who might not have access to the same amount of information as the well-funded, larger Northern NGOs. It also allowed for disputes to be dealt with within the NGO movement. An example of this was when one NGO caucus found that its 'leadership' had put out a statement without consultation and with all the organizational members of the caucus named on it. This resulted in one Canadian NGO being brought before its ambassador to explain why it had signed the statement, which it was, in fact, not in favour of. In this case, the NGOs concerned took the issue to the CSD NGO Steering Committee, and the caucus was closed down and put under steering committee responsibility until an election could be held to replace the former 'leadership'.

During the life of the steering committee (1994–2001), it had to take action in a further two caucuses due to complaints by its membership. The kind of recourse the steering committee could take included writing to the director of the NGO concerned, explaining what its staff had done.

Some people found the steering committee too rule-orientated, although it performed a very good service between meetings of the CSD. For example, it:

- maintained an up-to-date website;
- set up list servers for caucuses and maintained two general ones;
- acted as liaison with the UN for NGOs;
- sorted out accreditation problems;
- sorted out visa problems;
- raised funds for developing country NGO participation;

- managed preparation for CSD dialogue sessions;
- produced an annual report on the activities of the coalition;
- organized daily NGO sessions to report on developments in the negotiations;
- organized floor management for UN sessions with the caucuses.
- organized training for new NGOs;
- reached out to new NGOs to become involved in the CSD, especially when the issue was a new one – for example, tourism or transport;
- sorted out rooms for NGO meetings;
- organized press conferences;
- produced a diary of events that occurred during the CSD; and
- sorted out computer, internet and photocopying facilities.

Although it provided considerable services as a coalition, it did not survive for the ten-year review because of serious problems within it. It may be that NGO coalitions are not easy long-life bodies by the nature of the breadth of their membership.

There is an obvious problem that if there is no overall coalition for an issue, then NGOs will face a real problem in presenting their ideas before governments early enough. The steering committee oversaw the five-year review of the Earth Summit at Rio and completed a comprehensive policy document, as well as focusing upon ten key issues that it wanted government action on. It also let governments have their thoughts well before the first PrepCom in 1997. Of these ten objectives, it achieved five (see the section 'NGO/Stakeholder Papers and Statements' in Chapter 4).

During the 2002 Johannesburg Summit process, a coalition did form; but it was always behind the discussion rather than in front of it. This saw few successes for the NGO coalition during the summit process.

NGO and stakeholder coalitions

Non-governmental organizations

There are numerous NGO coalitions. Some around the World Summit on Sustainable Development (WSSD) were non-permanent, although they were very active, such as the ECOequity coalition. Others are more permanent, including the following.

Sustainable Development Issues Network (SDIN) The Sustainable Development Issues Network for 2002 is a collaborative effort among civil society networks and non-governmental issue caucuses aiming to improve communication and access to information on sustainable development issues. In particular, the initiative aims to improve communications among NGOs engaging in the World Summit on Sustainable Development, drawing especially upon the internet (www.sdissues.net/SDIN), as well as person-to-person relationships, to share knowledge and organize for action.

The SDIN evolved out of discussions among NGO issue caucuses and Major Groups seeking methods and vehicles to increase their effectiveness in contributing to the global dialogue on sustainable development policy at the CSD and other relevant intergovernmental arenas.

The SDIN is not meant to compete with or replace the networking and organizing efforts of other NGO bodies; instead, it aims to assist and promote the efforts of civil society networks working on sustainable development issues in various fora. In this sense, SDIN is not another 'network' per se but, hopefully, a useful tool of NGO networks.

This body is coordinated by three NGO coalitions: the Northern Alliance for Sustainability (ANPED), Environmental Liaison Centre International (ELCI) and Third World Network.

Networks around the Commission for Social Development (CSocD) There are a number of key networks that work around the CSocD. These are:

- International Council for Social Welfare (www.icsw.org);
- Social Watch: an NGO watchdog that monitors commitments made at Copenhagen (www.socwatch.org.uy);
- Oxfam International (www.oxfam.org).

Networks around the Commission on the Status of Women

- Energia: a global network on gender and energy (www.energia.org);
- The Gender and Water Alliance (www.genderandwateralliance.org);
- Woman's Human Rights Net: works in both human rights and women's commissions (www.whrNET.org);
- Women's International Coalition for Economic Justice (www.wicej.org);
- Women's Caucus around the Commission on Sustainable Development (www.earthsummit2002.org/wcaucus/csdngo.htm);
- Women's Environment and Development Organization (www.wedo.org).

Networks around the Commission on Human Settlements

- Habitat International: a network for housing and land rights (www.hic-mena.org);
- Huairou Commission: a network of grassroots women's organizations working on partnerships to create sustainable communities (www.huairou.org).

Networks working on human rights Important NGOs with Geneva offices working on the Commission on Human Rights (CHR) include:

- International Service for Human Rights: services NGOs attending the CHR (www.ishr.ch);
- Churches Commission on International Affairs: part of the World Council of Churches;
- Quaker office in Geneva;
- Women's International League for Peace and Freedom;
- Amnesty International (www.amnesty.org);
- Human Rights Watch (www.hrw.org).

Other human rights organizations active at the CHR are:

- Anti-Slavery International (www.antislavery.org);
- Article 19, the Global Campaign for Free Expression (www.article19.org);
- Human Rights International Alliance (www.hria.org);
- Human Rights and Peace Campaign (HURPEC) (http://hurpeconline.com);
- Institute for Human Rights and Development (www.africaninstitute.org).

Business and industry

Business Action for Sustainable Development (BASD)

BASD is a comprehensive network of business organizations that came together as a focus for the business contribution to the World Summit on Sustainable Development (WSSD) in 2002. BASD is a joint initiative of the International Chamber of Commerce (ICC) and the World Business Council for Sustainable Development (WBCSD). Guidance is provided by a small international steering committee under the leadership of Sir Mark Moody-Stuart. (http://basd.free.fr).

The BASD was created in 2001 with three goals:[4]

1   To ensure that the voice of business is heard in the preparations for the WSSD.
2   To identify where business can play a constructive role in the development and delivery of a sustainable future. BASD will emphasize business solutions to sustainable development that focus on concrete actions and deliverable results.
3   To demonstrate that business is already actively engaged in initiatives and partnerships to promote sustainable development.

International Chamber of Commerce (ICC)[5]

ICC is the voice of world business – championing the global economy as a force for economic growth, job creation and prosperity. Because national economies are now so closely interwoven, government decisions have far stronger international repercussions than in the past.

ICC – the world's only truly global business organization – responds by being more assertive in expressing business views. ICC activities cover a broad spectrum, from arbitration and dispute resolution to making the case for open trade and the market economy system, business self-regulation, fighting corruption or combating commercial crime.

ICC has direct access to national governments all over the world through its national committees. The organization's Paris-based international secretariat feeds business views into intergovernmental organizations on issues that directly affect business operations (www.iccwbo.org).

World Business Council on Sustainable Development (WBCSD)[6]

The WBCSD is a coalition of 160 international companies united by a shared commitment to sustainable development via the three pillars of economic growth, ecological balance and social progress. Members are drawn from more than 30 countries and 20 major industrial sectors. They also benefit from a global network of 40 national and regional business councils and partner organizations involving some 1000 business leaders globally.

The WBCSD was formed in January 1995 through a merger between the Business Council for Sustainable Development (BCSD) in Geneva and the World Industry Council for the Environment (WICE) in Paris. Since then, it has become the pre-eminent business voice on sustainable development issues and is playing a leading role in shaping business's response to the challenges of sustainable development.

The WBCSD mission is to provide business leadership as a catalyst for change toward sustainable development, and to promote the role of eco-efficiency, innovation and corporate social responsibility (www.wbcsd.org).

World Economic Forum

The World Economic Forum is an independent international organization committed to improving the state of the world. The forum provides a collaborative framework for the world's leaders to address global issues, particularly engaging its corporate members in global citizenship (www.weforum.org).

Children and youth

There are many different organizations that are active in the area of youth and children. Two good contacts are:

United Nations Association in Canada
Tel: +1 613 232 5751
www.youth2002jeunesse.unac.org

Leif Holmberg
Facilitator for Youth during WSSD
Tel: +46 70 229 2425
leif.holmberg@lsu.se
www.youth.se

AIESEC

AIESEC is the world's largest student organization. It is a global network of 50,000 members across more than 85 countries and territories at more than 800 universities worldwide. Each year, AIESEC facilitates international exchange of thousands of students and recent graduates throughout traineeships for non-profit organizations (www.aiesec.org).

European Youth Forum

The European Youth Forum is an international organization established by national youth councils and international non-

governmental youth organizations. It has incorporated the Youth
Forum of the European Union (YFEU), which acts as a bridge between
the European Youth Forum and the institutions of the European Union.
The European Youth Forum endeavours to serve the interests of young
people from all over Europe, promoting their active participation in
the construction of a common Europe and seeking to involve young
people in shaping a Europe based on the values of human rights,
democracy and mutual understanding (www.youthforum.org).

Peacechild International[7]

Peacechild International empowers children to take responsibility for
peace, human rights and the environment through education,
leadership development and direct participation in the events that
shape our world community. It does this through producing
publications, musicals, conferences and encouraging its affiliate youth
groups throughout the world.

Since 1990 the organization has focused its attention on
environmental issues. It has published three books with the UN. It has
launched the Rescue Mission Network, which is a project of Peacechild
International, and is devoted to implementing Agenda 21 and
sustainable development (www.peacechild.org).

South Eastern European Youth Council (SEEYC)

The main aim of SEEYC is to establish a platform for NGO cooperation
in the region of South-Eastern European (SEE) countries to work
toward the exchange of ideas and experiences in developing
democratic civil society. However, the basis for establishing this
integration lies in common characteristics and problems of young
people in the region (www.seeyc.org).

Youth for Habitat International Network[8]

Youth for Habitat International Network is an umbrella organization
operating at the international level through a secretariat with focal
points and resource persons in every region. It was created with the
aim of coordinating youth participation in the UN Conference on
Human Settlements. Youth Association for Habitat and Agenda 21
(YFHIN-Turkey) serves as the secretariat of the network and
implements projects for Habitat Agenda and Agenda 21 at the national
level (www.youthforhab.org.tr).

Farmers

There are two organizations that coordinate for farmers.

International Federation of Agricultural Producers (IFAP)[9]

IFAP was established in 1946 to secure the fullest cooperation between organizations of agricultural producers in meeting the optimum nutritional and consumptive requirements of the peoples of the world. It works to improve the economic and social status of all who live by and on the land (www.ifap.org).

Via Campesina[10]

Via Campesina is a movement of peasant and farm organizations from all of the alternative areas of the world, and is committed to solidarity and determination to move forward in the defence of people of the land (www.virtualsask.com/via).

Indigenous peoples

Earth Council[11]

The Earth Council runs an indigenous peoples website. The Indigenous and Tribal Peoples Centre of the Earth Council and its partners are working to enhance the capacity of its constituency to contribute to the construction of a sustainable and equitable future for all by generating concrete actions and results. An important aspect of its work is to find ways to perpetuate and combine traditional values, knowledge and practices by combining it with mainstream science, technology and education (www.earthcouncil.ac.cr).

Indigenous Environmental Network[12]

The Indigenous Environmental Network is an alliance of grassroots indigenous peoples whose mission is to protect the sacredness of the Earth from contamination and exploitation by strengthening, maintaining and respecting traditional teachings and natural laws (www.ienearth.org).

Tebtebba Foundation[13]

Tebtebba Foundation, the Indigenous Peoples' International Centre for Policy Research and Education, was established in 1996. Tebtebba, 'discourse' from the Philippine indigenous Kankanaey dialect, is firmly committed to the recognition, protection and promotion of indigenous peoples' rights worldwide.

Tebtebba's main thrust is to help build the capacity of indigenous peoples to assert their rights and articulate their own analyses and perspectives on issues directly affecting them (www.tebtebba.org).

Local authorities and regions

International Council for Local Environmental Initiatives (ICLEI)[14]

ICLEI is the international environmental agency for local governments. ICLEI's mission is to build and serve a worldwide movement of local governments to achieve tangible improvements in global environmental and sustainable development conditions through cumulative local actions.

Building a worldwide movement requires that ICLEI functions as a democratic, international association of local governments; it also operates as an international environmental agency for local governments.

More than 350 cities, towns, counties and their associations from around the world are full members of the council, with hundreds of additional local governments participating in specific ICLEI campaigns and projects. As a movement, association and agency, ICLEI continues to work towards its sustainable development goals. It tends to represent local government in the Commission on Sustainable Development (www.iclei.org).

International Union of Local Authorities (IULA)[15]

IULA was set up in 1913 and has membership in over 110 countries. It is the main local government body whose mission is to promote and unite democratic local government worldwide.

The strategic objectives of IULA are to:

- develop and maintain a strong democratic political organization, managed to high professional standards in a global setting;
- be the worldwide advocate and voice of democratic local government;
- be the worldwide source of key information and intelligence regarding democratic local government; and
- be the worldwide source of learning, exchange and capacity-building programmes for democratic local government (www.iula.org).

Network for Regional Governments for Sustainable Development (NRG4SD)[16]

Representatives of 22 regional governments from the five continents of the world, and several associations of regions, met together in Johannesburg on 31 August 2002 to confirm their common purpose in making sustainable development the central guiding principle of their governments, and to join together in a new global partnership network to share experience and enhance their separate ability to help their citizens achieve more sustainable futures. The outcome is known as the Network for Regional Governments for Sustainable Development (NRG4SD).

During the meeting the participants, who included several regional premiers, ministers, governors and other political leaders from the regions, agreed a political declaration – The Gauteng Declaration – which set out their shared purpose and declared their determination to adopt or strengthen existing overarching strategies to drive the progress of sustainable development in their regions.

The regional governments represented at the meeting also decided to establish a global network to exchange information, encourage the formation of partnerships and other forms of collaboration, and to clarify the roles of regional governments throughout the world in the pursuit of sustainable development. At this time, Stakeholder Forum acts as the interim secretariat. The network offers an interesting missing link in dealing with government, which has powers to deliver many of the commitments in the plans of actions as they are closer to the people and have substantial powers in many cases (www.nrg4sd.net).

United Cities and Local Government[17]

A new organization, United Cities and Local Governments, is to be created as a result of the unification of IULA and the United Towns Organization (UTO). It will commence operations on 1 January 2004, with its headquarters in Barcelona, Spain.

The mission of United Cities and Local Governments is 'to be the united voice and world advocate of democratic local self-government, promoting its values, objectives and interests, through cooperation between local governments, and within the wider international community'.

United Cities and Local Governments will ensure the effective political representation of local government to the international community, will promote international cooperation between local governments and their associations, and will be the worldwide source of key information regarding local government.

World Associations of Cities and Local Authorities Coordination (WACLAC)[18]

The important link between local government and the UN is coordinated at the international level through WACLAC. WACLAC is a world alliance of international associations of cities and local authorities and its members include IULA, UTO, Metropolis and the Arab Towns Organization (ATO).

WACLAC was created following the World Assembly of Cities and Local Authorities during the Istanbul Conference on Human Settlements in 1996. This conference placed great importance on the role of local government and increased the necessity for better coordination at the global level (www.waclac.org).

Scientific and technological community

International Council for Scientific Union (ICSU)[19]

ICSU is a non-governmental organization, founded in 1931 to bring together natural scientists in international scientific endeavour. It comprises 98 multi-disciplinary national scientific members (scientific research councils or science academies) and 26 international, single-discipline scientific unions to provide a wide spectrum of scientific expertise enabling members to address major international interdisciplinary issues that none could handle alone. ICSU also has 28 scientific associates.

The council seeks to break the barriers of specialization by initiating and coordinating major international interdisciplinary programmes and by creating interdisciplinary bodies, which undertake activities and research programmes of interest to several members. A number of bodies set up within ICSU also address matters of common concern to all scientists, such as capacity-building in science, environment and development and the free conduct of science.

The council acts as a focus for the exchange of ideas and information and the development of standards. Hundreds of congresses, symposia and other scientific meetings are organized each year around the world, and a wide range of newsletters, handbooks and journals is published (www.icsu.org).

Trade unions

International Confederation of Free Trade Unions (ICFTU)[20]

ICFTU was set up in 1949 and has 231 affiliated organizations in 150 countries and territories on all five continents, with a membership of 158 million.

It has three major regional organizations: the Asian and Pacific Regional Organisation (ICFTU-APRO), the African Regional Organisation (ICFTU-AFRO), and the Inter-American Regional Organisation of Workers (ICFTU-ORIT). It also maintains close links with the European Trade Union Confederation (which includes all ICFTU European affiliates) and Global Union Federations that link together national unions from a particular trade or industry at international level.

The ICFTU cooperates closely with the International Labour Organization (ILO) and has consultative status with the UN Economic and Social Council (ECOSOC) and with specialized agencies, such as the UN Educational, Scientific and Cultural Organization (UNESCO) and the Food and Agriculture Organization (FAO) (www.icftu.org).

Women

There are many women's organizations that are involved in the UN. The following provides a list of some of the better known ones:

Energia
www.energia.org

Gender and Water Alliance
www.genderandwateralliance.org

Women's Caucus around the Commission on Sustainable Development
www.earthsummit2002.org/wcaucus/csdngo.htm

Women's Environment and Development Organization
www.wedo.org

Woman's Human Rights Net
www.whrNET.org

Women's International Coalition for Economic Justice
www.wicej.org

Chapter 7

UN Commissions and Conferences[1]

UN COMMISSIONS

The UN commissions usually meet annually and enable governments and stakeholders to review progress towards agreed outcomes and to develop new areas of policy, or just update old areas.

Commission on Human Settlements

The Commission on Human Settlements (CHS) undertakes the mandate of the UN Human Settlements Programme (UN-Habitat), promoting the Habitat Agenda. UN-Habitat has the following mission statement:

> The mission of UN-Habitat is to promote sustainable urbanization through policy formulation, institutional reform, capacity-building, technical cooperation and advocacy, and to monitor and improve the state of human settlements worldwide.

UN-Habitat was formerly the UN Centre for Human Settlements (Habitat). It was originally founded in 1978 after the first UN Conference on Human Settlements (also known as Habitat), held in 1976. It has been the UN focal point for work on human settlement issues since then. The second UN Conference on Human Settlements

(Habitat II) in Istanbul in 1996 started a process that resulted in the UN General Assembly on 26 February 2002 upgrading the centre to a UN programme, as well as upgrading the commission from a standing committee to a full UN Economic and Social Council (ECOSOC) subsidiary commission.

At the five-year review of Habitat II, ECOSOC agreed that the programme would focus on two areas:

1   the Global Campaign for Secure Tenure;
2   the Global Campaign on Urban Governance.

The commission has a membership of 58, which is made up of 16 seats from Africa, 13 from Asia, 6 from Eastern Europe, ten from Latin America and the Caribbean, and 13 from Western Europe and other states. When elected, they serve for a four-year term. The commission acts as the governing body for UN-Habitat and provides policy guidance and direction supervision.

UN-Habitat also oversees two key outreach campaigns. These are:

1   World Habitat Day (annually on the first Monday in October);
2   the Urban Forum, which offers an opportunity for those involved in sustainable urbanization to share experiences.

UN-Habitat has pioneered the involvement of stakeholders in developing policy and the advice given to governments. During the 1996 Habitat II conference, it brought out the NGO suggested text amendments as an official UN information document and allowed NGOs and local authorities the opportunity to present suggested amendments during the negotiations. If a government took up these suggestions, they became active during the negotiations. It may be because Habitat II was at the end of the original 1990s conference series that it greatly benefited from the advances made in other conferences.

UN-Habitat
PO Box 30030
Nairobi 00100
Kenya
Tel: +254 2 621 234
Fax: +254 2 624 266/267
Email: habitat@unhabitat.org
www.unhabitat.org

Contact for NGO/stakeholder relations: Anantha Krishnan
(anantha.krishnan@unhabitat.org)

Commission on Population and Development

The Commission on Population was originally established in October
1946. It was modified as a result of the International Conference on
Population and Development (ICPD) in 1994, becoming the
Commission on Population and Development (CPD). The UN General
Assembly directed the commission to monitor, review and assess the
implementation of the programme of action of the conference. The
programme is designed to guide national and international policies on
population and development over the next 20 years. In addition, the
assembly requested other specialized agencies to implement and
adjust their work programmes in line with the provisions under the
programme of action of the conference.

The commission is made up of 47 member states. These are 12
from Africa, 11 from Asia, 5 from Eastern Europe, 9 from Latin America
and 10 from Western Europe and other states. They are elected for
terms of four years.

The commission coordinates its activities through a system of
topic-orientated multi-year work programmes. These are assessed via
a five-yearly review of the progress made in the implementation of the
programme of action.

The UN Population Division services the commission, which is part
of the Department of Economic and Social Affairs (DESA). The director
of the division is Joseph Chamie. It also helps facilitate access by
governments to 'information trends and their inter-relationships with
social and economic development as an input to government policy
and programme formulations'. It also 'enhances coordination and
cooperation among organizations of the UN'.

For further information on the commission, refer to:

Population Division
Department of Economic and Social Affairs
2 UN Plaza
Room DC2–1950
United Nations
New York
NY 10017
Tel: +1 212 963 3179
Fax: +1 212 963 2147

www.un.org/esa/population/unpop.htm
Contact for NGO/stakeholder relations: Michele Fedoroff
(fedoroff@un.org)

Commission for Social Development

The Commission for Social Development (CSocD) is a long-standing commission in the UN. It was set up in 1946 and has become the main monitoring place for the implementation of the World Summit for Social Development, held in Copenhagen in 1995. The Copenhagen summit was the largest gathering of world leaders at that time. It pledged to make the conquest of poverty, the goal of full employment and the fostering of social integration overriding objectives of development.

The commission meets annually and has 46 members: 12 from Africa, 10 from Asian states, 9 from Latin America, 5 from Eastern Europe and 10 from Western Europe and other states.

The Division for Social Policy and Development, which is housed in DESA, oversees the commission:

Division for Social Policy and Development
Department of Economic and Social Affairs
2 United Nations Plaza
Room DC2–1360
United Nations
New York
NY 10017
Tel: +1 212 963 3175
Fax: +1 212 963 3062
Email: social@un.org.
www.un.org/esa/socdev
Contact for NGO/stakeholder relations: Yao N'Goran (ngoran@un.org)

To attend a meeting, send a letter to the above contact. An invitation letter is available online at www.un.org/esa/socdev/ngo/index.htlm.

Commission on Sustainable Development

The Commission on Sustainable Development (CSD) was set up in 1993 in the aftermath of the Earth Summit. The CSD monitors the implementation of Agenda 21 and the outcomes from the five-year review – the UN General Assembly Special Session (UNGASS or Rio +5) in 1997. It will also be likely to monitor the outcomes of the ten-year review – the World Summit on Sustainable Development (WSSD or Earth Summit 2002) held in Johannesburg.

The commission has 53 members: 13 from African states, 11 from Asian states, 6 from Eastern Europe, 10 from Latin America and the Caribbean, and 13 from Western Europe and other states. The commission has been a favourite one with governments. In 1996, the UK environment minister, John Gummer took the unusual action of writing to all of his other ministerial colleagues requesting that the UK be re-elected to the commission for another term – which occurred. For the bureau of the ten-year review, Germany and Sweden could not agree within the Western Europe and other states group who should be on the bureau and the election was taken to a full vote, not of the CSD but the membership of the UN. This occurred because the 10th session of the CSD (CSD 10) was acting as the PrepCom for the WSSD.

The Division on Sustainable Development acted as the secretariat to the WSSD and services the CSD. It is also part of DESA. In addition to the work that it does for the CSD, it services related areas, such as forests in the UN Forest Forum, and the outcomes from the UN Small Island Developing States Conference. The technical support section works in the areas of mineral resources, freshwater management, energy, and infrastructure and land management:

Division for Sustainable Development
Department of Economic and Social Affairs
2 UN Plaza
Room DC2–2220
United Nations
New York
NY 10017
Tel: +1 212 963 3170
Fax: +1 212 963 4260
Email: dsd@un.org
www.un.org/esa/sustdev
Contact for NGO/stakeholder relations: Zehra Aydin-Sipos
(aydin@un.org)

To attend a commission meeting, contact Zehra Aydin-Sipos. Guidelines on how to proceed are found online at www.un.org/esa/sustdev.

Commission on Human Rights

The United Nations Commission on Human Rights was set up in 1946 and 'reports regarding the international bill of rights, international declarations or conventions on civil liberties, the status of women, freedom of information and similar matters, the protection of minorities, the prevention of discrimination on the basis of race, sex, language or religion, and other mater concerning human rights'.

The commission has 53 members, made up of 15 from Africa, 12 from Asia, 5 from Eastern Europe, 11 from Latin America and the Caribbean, and 10 from Western Europe and other states.

The commission has probably the most active attendance from NGOs of all of the commissions. It also lasts the longest – around six weeks – and spends much time looking at the implementation of human rights agreements. The commission receives information from governmental organizations and individuals in the preparation of reports.

The commission has a sub-commission, which consists of expert individuals who do not represent the views of their governments. However, some members appear as individual experts at one session and as government delegates at the next, casting doubt on their independence. The sub-commission carries out studies on human rights issues and receives reports on country situations. It makes recommendations on which countries' records should be considered at the commission itself. This irritates certain countries and there is pressure to limit the powers of the sub-commission.

The secretariat for the commission is the Office of the High Commissioner for Human Rights:

Office of the High Commissioner for Human Rights
United Nations Office in Geneva
Palais Wilson
Avenue de la Paix 8–14
1211 Genève 10
Tel: +41 22 917 9000
Fax: +41 22 917 90 11
Email: 1503@ohchr.org
www.unhchr.ch

Commission on the Status of Women

The Commission on the Status of Women was set up in 1946 and monitors the implementation of the 1995 Beijing Platform of Action; it also looks at women's rights, in general.

The commission has, in total, 45 members, elected for four-year terms. There are 13 African members, 11 from Asia, 4 from Eastern Europe, 9 from Latin America and the Caribbean and 8 from Western Europe and other states.

The Division on the Status of Women acts as the focal point for coordination and mainstreaming of gender issues within the UN system. It conducts research in the 12 areas covered by the Beijing Platform of Action and serves as the secretariat of the commission. The mission statement of the division is:

> *Grounded in the vision of equality of the United Nations Charter, the division advocates the improvement of the status of women of the world and the achievement of their equality with men. It aims to ensure the participation of women as equal partners with men in all aspects of human endeavour. It promotes women as equal participants and beneficiaries of sustainable development, peace and security, governance and human rights. It strives to stimulate the mainstreaming of a gender perspective both within and outside the UN system.*

The division also assists the Committee on the Elimination of Discrimination against Women (CEDAW). Carolyn Hannan was appointed as director of the Division for the Advancement of Women in 2001.

United Nations Division for the Advancement of Women
2 UN Plaza
New York
NY 10017
Tel: +1 212 963 3169
Fax: +1 212 963 3463
Email: daw@un.org
www.un.org/womenwatch/daw
Contact for NGO/stakeholder relations: Amina Adam

UN Conferences and Summits

As a confirmed UN conference and summit groupie, I think that they are vital events to enable the world to set new norms and standards to address the key issues of the day.

They can be attacked by the press as a waste of money. It is difficult to think of another way in which such diverse cultures and political viewpoints might try to address issues that, in many cases, are national and not international, and where they are being judged by their peer group on what they have and have not done, or are prepared to do.

UN Conference on Environment and Development (UNCED), Rio de Janiero, 1992

For all intents and purposes, the road began with the Earth Summit in Rio de Janeiro in 1992. This meeting was unprecedented for a UN conference in terms of both the size and scope of concerns. Leaders of nations from around the globe (172 governments represented, 108 by heads of state) joined together with 2400 NGO representatives in search of ways to help governments rework economic development strategy, to eliminate the destruction of natural resources and to reduce pollution on the planet. In other words, the conference centred around making the necessary decisions needed to ensure a healthy planet for future generations.

In 1972, at the UN Conference on the Human Environment in Stockholm, the relationship between economic development and the environment was recognized for the first time and, in turn, was placed on the international agenda. As a result of this conference, the UN Environment Programme (UNEP) was founded in order to act as a motivational tool for action to protect the environment. Despite this new programme, very little was done in the years to come to integrate environmental concerns within the areas of national economic planning and decision-making. In 1983, environmental degradation was on its way to absurdity in developing nations and, in turn, the UN set up the World Commission on Environment and Development. Finally, in 1987 the UN General Assembly called for the UN Conference on Environment and Development (UNCED). The primary goals of the summit included: the establishment of concrete strategies that would ensure broad-based sustainable development; and forming foundations for global partnerships between the developing and the industrialized worlds while focusing on mutual needs and common interests of both, thus ensuring a healthy future for the planet.

The Earth Summit held its central concern as being the need for broad-based, environmentally sustainable development. The issues included, but were not limited to, the adoption of Agenda 21, a comprehensive programme of action to attain sustainable development on the global scale; patterns of production, particularly the production of toxic components; alternative sources of energy to replace the use of fossil fuels; and awareness of, and concern over, the growing scarcity of water.

After discussion of these and other issues, 108 governments adopted three major agreements concerned with changing the traditional approach to development:

1   the Rio Declaration on Environment and Development (a series of principles defining the rights and responsibilities of states);
2   the Statement of Forest Principles (a set of principles to underline the sustainable management of forests worldwide); and
3   Agenda 21.

In addition, two legally binding conventions, the United Nations Framework Convention on Climate Change and the Convention on Biological Diversity (CBD), both seeking, respectively, to prevent global climate change and the eradication of the diversity of biological species, were opened for signature at the summit, providing a forum for the development of these issues.

As a result of the summit and these agreements, three bodies were created within the UN to ensure full support for implementation of Agenda 21 and other programmes worldwide. These bodies included the CSD; the Inter-Agency Committee on Sustainable Development (IACSD); and the High-level Advisory Board on Sustainable Development. The Earth Summit has influenced all of the proceeding major UN conferences, which have dealt with the relationships between human rights, population, social development, women and human settlements, and the need for environmentally sustainable development. For example, the World Conference on Human Rights, held in Vienna in 1993, underscored the right of people to a healthy environment and the right to development, controversial demands that had met with resistance from some member states prior to the Earth Summit.

World Conference on Human Rights, Vienna, 1993

Starting with the Universal Declaration of Human Rights in 1948, the UN articulated an international code of human rights based on those rights that are absolutely necessary to our survival and without which we cannot live fully as human beings. These include, but are not limited to, a broad range of internationally accepted rights in civil, cultural, economic, political and social areas. The UN also established effective mechanisms with which to promote and protect these rights, while assisting governments in carrying out their responsibilities.

In 1989, the UN General Assembly called for a second world meeting (the first was in Tehran in 1968) that would review and assess progress made in the field of human rights since the adoption of the Universal Declaration in 1948. When this second conference was called, there was an overwhelming sense that human rights needed to be better integrated within the overall policies and programmes promoting economic and social development, democratic structures and peacekeeping. In this sense, Vienna was a reflection of a commitment reached by the international community to address human rights issues.

The second World Conference on Human Rights, which took place in Vienna in June 1993, marked the first major world review of human rights. The conference brought together 7000 participants, including an unprecedented number of government delegates from 171 countries; representatives from UN treaty bodies, academia and national institutions; and representatives of more than 800 NGOs. The principal theme of the conference was the promotion and protection of human rights as the birthright of all human beings and the responsibility of governments at all levels. The resulting document of the conference was the Vienna Declaration and Programme of Action, which outlines a comprehensive plan for strengthening the implementation of human rights and focuses on the links between development, government and the promotion of human rights.

During the conference, issues centred around the promotion and protection of human rights, and the Vienna Declaration and Programme of Action was adopted. This underscored the universality of human rights as the birthright of all human beings and the first responsibility of all governments involved. It also addressed other issues concerned with the legitimacy of development and the protection of vulnerable groups (such as women, children, indigenous people and refugees), and pointed out that extreme poverty and social exclusion are violations of human dignity, thus requiring that the state foster poverty eradication and participation by the poorest members of society. Furthermore, as a result of the knowledge and information highlighted by the conference, the UN General Assembly proclaimed, in 1994, the UN Decade for Human Rights (1995–2004), which promotes awareness and encourages the establishment of national and international committees composed of representatives from the public and private sector. In the end, the UN Secretary-General Boutros Boutros-Ghali told the delegates of the conference that by adopting the Vienna Declaration and Programme of Action, they had renewed the international community's commitment to the promotion and protection of human rights and saluted the meeting for having forged 'a new vision for global action for human rights into the next century'.

International Conference on Population and Development, Cairo, 1994

The International Conference on Population and Development (ICPD), held in Cairo in September 1994, witnessed the development of new strategies that focus on meeting the needs of individual men and women, rather than only target groups. Those attending the conference included representatives from 179 governments and over 1500 NGOs from 113 countries, gathered in order to discuss issues centred around population, sustainable development and economic growth. The result of these discussions was the programme of action of the ICPD, an outline of procedures that would guide both national and international policies on population and development for the following 20 years.

During the World Population Conference, held in Bucharest in 1974, the issues concerned with population were fully addressed by the international community and a World Population Plan of Action was established. This plan provided principle objectives concerning economic and social development in the realm of population. The principles included, but were not limited to, the following:

- The formulation of population policies is the independent right of each nation.
- Any individual has the right to freely decide the number of children that they have, along with the information and educational means to aid in the decision.
- Population and development are coincidental.

The following International Conference on Population, held in Mexico City in 1984, adopted many recommendations regarding the plan, with a central focus on the need to improve the status of women and provide universal access to family planning methods. As a result, this modified version of the plan would serve as the basis for the discussions held at the ICPD in Cairo.

After discussion, the ICPD formulated the programme of action, which provides an outline for all people to become aware of ways to enhance their own, and their children's, health and well-being. This plan of action recognizes the coincidences between population and development and aspires to make evident to everyone their reproductive rights, including the right of access to family planning practices and the right to determine the amount of children that they wish to have. The three main goals set by the programme included:

1 making family planning universally available by 2015 in order to reduce infant and maternity mortality rates;
2 integrating population concerns within all policies in the realm of sustainable development; and
3 making available to women and girls the opportunities for education, health and employment services in order to provide them with more options.

In the end, the programme set goals in three areas that would guide both national and international policies on development and population for the 20 years to come, thus making it a major point on the road to 2002 and sustainable development.

The World Summit for Social Development, Copenhagen, 1995

In March 1995, the World Summit for Social Development was held in Copenhagen, Denmark, making the promotion of a people-centred plan for social development evident to the governments of the world. The summit was attended by representatives from 186 governments, with 117 represented by heads of state; 2315 representatives from 811 NGOs were also present. Discussions at the summit were centred around the issues of poverty eradication, social integration and the reduction of unemployment with the promotion of productive employment. As a result of these discussions, the Copenhagen Declaration on Social Development and its programme of action were drafted and endorsed by all states in attendance, representing the largest consensus on social development issues ever reached at the international level.

The Copenhagen summit was held as a result of the growing international concern with social development problems, specifically dealing with poverty and social disintegration, conflict and insecurity. These problems became evident to both rich and poor and, in turn, promoted a great concern for solutions. These solutions, being out of any single government's reach, were not easily accessible and not usually socially and economically balanced. As a result, the summit had as one of its primary goals to make evident ways of doing away with such imbalances by placing social development back on the international agenda.

After the discussions at the summit, and after both the Declaration on Social Development and the programme of action were adopted, the issue was, most definitely, back on the table. The declaration established ten commitments, with each followed by a method of action. A sample of these commitments included eradicating poverty through national action and international cooperation; giving priority to the rights and needs of vulnerable groups (such as women, children and indigenous people); the promotion of full and freely chosen employment; the promotion of universal access to education and health care; the promotion of social integration through the protection of human rights and respect for cultural, ethnic and religious diversity; and the promotion of equity between women and men. Other results of the conference included the UN General Assembly establishing the International Year for the Eradication of Poverty (1996) as a way of promoting a heightened awareness of poverty and encouraging action on a global scale. A decade with this same focus was also established and began in 1997. The summit was deemed the nexus of a series of global conferences concerning social development and, in turn, has influenced the policy-making process for a new era.

The World Conference on Women, Beijing, 1995

The 1995 World Conference on Women, held in Beijing, brought together almost 50,000 men and women from across the globe to discuss gender issues. Included in this number were 189 governments and 5000 representatives from 2100 NGOs with 30,000 individuals attending the independent NGO Forum 1995. The conference was centred around, but not limited to, the themes of the advancement and empowerment of women in relation to women's human rights; women and poverty; women and decision-making; the girl child; and violence against women. The resulting document was the Beijing Declaration and Platform for Action, which, among other things, set out measures for national and international action for the advancement of women over the five years until 2000.

The motive to hold the Fourth World Conference on Women stemmed primarily from the momentum generated by the three previous women's conferences (Mexico City, 1975; Copenhagen, 1980; and Nairobi, 1985) and also from the United Nations Decade for Women (1976–1985). All of these movements gave international awareness to, and support for, national and international women's groups around the globe, while influencing the series of world conferences from the Children's Summit in New York (where the special needs of the girl child were addressed); to the Earth Summit in Rio (where the need for acknowledgement of women's central role in sustainable development was emphasized); to the Human Rights Conference in Vienna (where the equal rights of women was recognized); to the World Summit for Social Development in Copenhagen (which addressed the central role that women have to play in combating poverty); to Cairo and Istanbul (where women's right to exercise control over decisions affecting their health, families and homes was underscored). All of these meetings paved the way for the Beijing conference to reach the objectives of ensuring equality of women, preventing violence against women, and advancing their participation in efforts to promote peace, along with economic and political decision-making – areas where progress was lacking.

After discussion at the conference, the Beijing Declaration and Platform for Action was adopted. An example of the advances made in the platform include women's rights as human rights (recognizing violence against women as a human rights problem and also allowing women control over sexuality and reproductive health); reviewing laws containing punitive measures against women who have undergone illegal abortion; and recognizing rape as a war crime punishable by law. In the end, the overriding message of the conference was that the issues addressed in the platform for action are both global and universal. The conference recognized that, in countries across the globe, cultural traditions, attitudes and practices promote inequality and discrimination against women, in both public and private life. As a result, the conference realized that the implementation of the platform requires changes in values, attitudes practices and priorities at all levels. The conference supported a clear commitment to international standards, of which the equality between men and women is promoted, protected and measured with emphasis on the human rights of women and girl children. The recognition of this as an integral part of universal human rights, and mandating that institutions at all levels must be re-oriented to expedite its implementation, proved to be another major step on the road to 2002.

United Nations Conference on Human Settlements, Istanbul, 1996

The second UN Conference on Human Settlements (Habitat II or the City Summit), held in Istanbul in 1996, was one of the last in a cycle of major UN conferences that have shaped the global development agenda for years to come. The focus brought together issues that were dealt with at earlier conferences as they relate to the pressing problem of the rapid urbanization of today's world. Those attending the conference included representatives from 171 governments and an unprecedented 8000 people from 2400 NGOs (who were allowed access, for the first time, to participate in deliberations as full partners), and focused their discussions on the principal themes of sustainable human settlements development in the urbanizing world, with the provision of adequate shelter for all. As a result, the conference adopted the Habitat Agenda, a plan that provides an effective tool for creating sustainable human settlements for the next generation with regard to broad-based sustainable development (such as environmental, human rights, social development, women's and population issues) in the specific context of urbanization.

The first UN Conference on Human Settlement, in Vancouver in 1976, had sought to develop strategies to suppress the negative effects of rapid urbanization. Twenty years later, half of the world's population resides in cities, with the majority living in poverty. UN-Habitat serves as the nexus for human settlements development within the UN system, and also as the secretariat of both the CHS and Habitat II. In 1988, the UN General Assembly adopted the Global Strategy for Shelter to the Year 2000, emphasizing an enabling approach where governments do not provide shelter itself, but a coordinating legal institution and regulatory environment to motivate people to provide and improve upon their own living conditions. The Habitat II conference would review and evaluate this strategy and UN-Habitat (at that time, the UN Centre for Human Settlements), prompted by the Earth Summit in 1992 where it was made clear that 600 million people live in threatened housing conditions throughout the world.

During the conference, the participants agreed to address many important issues concerning human settlements, including unsustainable consumption and production patterns; unsustainable population changes; homelessness; unemployment; lack of basic infrastructure and services; growing insecurity and violence; and increased vulnerability to disasters. After discussion of the issues, the Habitat Agenda was formulated as an acting guide towards achieving broad-based sustainable development within the world's cities, towns and villages into the first two decades of the 21st century. Included within the agenda is a statement of goals, commitments and strategies for implementation. The goals within the agenda include poverty eradication; strengthening of the family; partnership among countries; and increased financial resources. The commitments cover adequate shelter for all, sustainable settlements, gender equality, financing of settlements, international cooperation, and the assessment of progress. The strategies emphasize that individuals, families and communities must be enabled to improve their housing, and that the government should promote better housing by prohibiting discrimination and ensuring legal security. Habitat II offered a positive vision of sustainable human settlements where all have shelter and a healthy and safe environment in which to live, with basic services provided.

World Food Summit, Rome, 1996

The World Food Summit, held in Rome in 1996, was the first global gathering of heads of state and government to address the problems of hunger and malnutrition, coming at a time when slowing growth of global food production was matched to an expanding world population. The purpose of the meeting was to establish a new concern in the fight for food security by focusing the attention of policy- and decision-makers in the public and private sectors on food issues. In attendance were 186 governments, including 41 represented by presidents, 15 by vice presidents and 41 by prime ministers, not to mention many representatives from the NGO community. The conference was focused around food security and participants renewed their commitment to ensuring that everyone in the world had sufficient access to nutritious food in order for survival and a healthy life. The summit adopted the Rome Declaration and the World Food Summit Plan of Action, which outline methods to achieve universal food security and to reduce, by half, the current number of undernourished people in developing countries by 2015.

The World Food Conference, held in Rome in 1974, first addressed the issue of food security on a worldwide scale. It took place during a time when food reserves were diminishing and governments proclaimed that 'every man, woman and child has the inalienable right to be free from hunger and malnutrition in order to develop their physical and mental faculties'. With goals of eradicating hunger and establishing food security within a decade, considerable progress had been made; but goals were not met. This promoted a deep concern about global food insecurity and, in turn, prompted the Food and Agricultural Organization (FAO) to call a World Food Summit of government heads to address the growing problems of world hunger and food insecurity.

The resulting documents of the summit included both the Rome Declaration on World Food Security and the World Food Summit Plan of Action. The plan of action outlines seven commitments to be carried out on the part of participating governments. These commitments are expected to aid significantly in the fight to eradicate hunger and are concerned with the areas of general conditions for economic and social progress to ensure food security; poverty eradication and access to food; sustainable increases in the production of food; contribution of trade to food security; preparedness, prevention and response to food emergencies; optimal investment in human resources and comprehensive sustainable development; and cooperation in the implementation and monitoring of the plan of action. In the end, the main goal of the summit remained: it was to reduce, by half, the number of malnourished people in the world by 2015.

Notes

PREFACE

1   Stakeholders in the context of the UN tend to be those identified in Agenda 21 as 'Major Groups', including women, youth and children, NGOs, local government, business and industry, trade unions, scientific and technological community, farmers and indigenous people. Others have been trying to gain a similar status, such as the education community, older people and the faith community.

KEY MESSAGES

1   Adapted from suggestions by Paul Hohnen.

CHAPTER 2

1   See Preface, Note 1
2   For a list of the Agenda 21 Major Groups, see Preface, Note 1.
3   Taken from Hemmati (2002).
4   PrepComs are formal UN meetings to prepare for a conference or summit. This is where most of the work happens.

CHAPTER 3

1   Stakeholder Forum published *Earth Summit 2002: A New Deal* in late 2000 (revised edition, Dodds with Middleton, 2001), which identified some of the key political agenda issues for the summit and the challenges in front of us. The Danish government, in preparation for the European PrepCom in September 2001, used the term 'a New Deal' to indicate the high ground possible for the WSSD in Johannesburg.

2   Stakeholder Forum has template resources that show how to review national progress on the chapters of Agenda 21. These can be found on the website www.stakeholderforum.org.

3   ECOSOC is one of the five permanent bodies that make up the UN. The others are the International Court of Justice, the UN General Assembly, the UN Security Council and the Trusteeship Council.

4   At the time of publication, the EU consists of Austria, Belgium, Denmark, Finland, France, Germany, Greece, Ireland, Italy, Luxembourg, The Netherlands, Portugal, Spain, Sweden and the UK. EU leaders have agreed to expand the bloc from 15 to 25 members in May 2004, taking in Cyprus, the Czech Republic, Estonia, Hungary, Latvia, Lithuania, Malta, Poland, Slovakia and Slovenia.

5   The *Earth Negotiations Bulletin* is an independent reporting service, published by the International Institute for Sustainable Development (IISD), that provides daily information in print and electronic formats from multilateral negotiations on environment and development. It can be accessed at www.iisd.ca/enbvol/enb-background.htm.

6   The issue was the institutional follow-up to the Habitat II Conference. Stakeholder Forum advocated that this should be through the Secretary-General's Administrative Committee for Coordination (ACC). The opposing view was that it should be through the Commission on Human Settlements. The reason for choosing the ACC is that it is the Coordinating Mechanism in the UN for joined-up thinking.

7   NGLS can be contacted via www.unsystem.org/ngls.

CHAPTER 4

1   A website for the CSD NGO Steering Committee exists at http://csdngo.igc.org but at the time this book went to press, their home page was 'under construction'. The information can also be accessed at http://csdngo.igc.org/sitemap.htm.

2   The six languages are Arabic, Chinese, English, French, Russian and Spanish.

3   This review has been adapted from de la Rosa (1999).

4   This was developed by Rosalie Gardiner, with help from Stakeholder Forum's international advisory board and staff.

5   Peter Hain MP is a former South African political exile who, at the time of publication, is a cabinet minister of the UK government.

6   These definitions have been taken from the UN website http://untreaty.un.org/english/guide.asp to ensure their accuracy.

7   Drawn from Fiona McConnell's (1996) explanation in *The Biodiversity Convention: A Negotiating History*. Fiona McConnell was vice chair of UNED-UK from 1993 to 1997, and before that was chief negotiator for the UK government in the Earth Summit preparatory process.

CHAPTER 5

1   Taken from the website www.conferencegeneva.com/tourist-board.htm.
2   These are a set of hotels used by NGOs around the UN.

CHAPTER 6

1   Jesse Jackson's quotes can be found on the websites www. brainyquote.com and www.famous-quotes-and-quotations.com.
2   Taken from the UN Geneva website www.unog.ch/genet/permis/ misset.htm, and added to by our research.
3   Taken from the book *Permanent Missions to the United Nations*, published twice yearly by the UN. The New York contact information is also available at www.un.org/Overview/missions.htm. For websites of the Permanent Missions to the UN, see www.un.int.
4   Taken from BASD website http://basd.free.fr.
5   Taken from the ICC website www.iccwbo.org.
6   Taken from the WBCSD website www.wbcsd.org.
7   Taken from the Peacechild website www.peacechild.org.
8   Taken from the Youth for Habitat website www.youthforhab.org.tr.
9   Taken from the IFAP website www.ifap.org.
10 Taken from the Via Campesina website www.virtualsask.com/via.
11 Taken from the Earth Council website www.earthcouncil.ac.cr.
12 Taken from the Indigenous Environmental Network website www. ienearth.org.
13 Taken from the Tebtebba website www.tebtebba.org.
14 Taken from the ICLEI website www.iclei.org.
15 Taken from the IULA website www.iula.org.
16 Taken from the NRG4SD website www.nrg4sd.net.
17 Taken from the IULA website www.iula.org.
18 Taken from the WACLAC website www.waclac.org.
19 Taken from the ICSU website www.icsu.org.
20 Taken from the ICFTU website www.icftu.org.

CHAPTER 7

1   This chapter has been developed from the Roadmap section of www.stakeholderforum.org, originally drawn up by Toby Middleton.

References

Alinsky, S (1971) *Rules for Radicals: A Practical Primer for Realistic Radicals*, Random House, New York

Carroll, L (1865) *Through the Looking Glass*, Penguin Books, London

de la Rosa, J (1999) 'Five Years and Beyond: Evaluating Implementation and Renewing Commitment', in Foster and Anand (eds) *Whose World is it Anyway?*, United Nations Association in Canada, Ottawa

Dodds, F, McCoy, M and Tanner S (1997) *Towards Earth Summit 2*, CSD NGO Steering Committee, New York

Dodds, F with Middleton, T (eds) (2001) *Earth Summit 2002: A New Deal*, Earthscan Publications, London

Elgin, S H (1994) *Earthsong: Native Tongue 3*, Daw Books, New York

Foster, J W and Anand A (eds) (1999) *Whose World Is It Anyway?: Civil Society, the United Nations and the Multilateral Future*, United Nations Association in Canada, Ottawa

Hain, P (1971) *Don't Play with Apartheid*, George Allen and Unwin, London

Hemmati, M (2002) *Multi-stakeholder Processes for Governance and Sustainability: Beyond Deadlock and Conflict*, Earthscan Publications, London

Hemmati, M and Seliger K (eds) (2001) *The Stakeholder Tool Kit: A Resource for Women and NGOs*, Stakeholder Forum, London

McConnell, F (1996) *The Biodiversity Convention: A Negotiating History*, Kluwer Law International, London

United Nations (1992) *Agenda 21*, UN, New York

Willetts, P (1999) 'The Rules of the Game: The United Nations and Civil Society', in Foster and Anand (eds) *Whose World is it Anyway?*, United Nations Association in Canada, Ottawa

Watzlawick, P, Beavin, M J and Jackson, D (1967) *Pragmatics of Human Communication: A Study of Interactional Patters, Pathologies and Paradoxes*, WW Norton, New York

Index